W9-CES-637

Written by the staff of Ortho Books, in association with the consultants listed at left.

Written by
Michael MacCaskey

Contributing Editor
Lance Walheim

Edited by
Scott R. Millard

Photography by
William Aplin
Michael Landis

Illustrations by
Ebet Dudley

All About
LAWNS

Contents

Lawns of North America

Regionalized for 12 southern states, answering the most frequently asked questions about growing lawns.

We think this book will be more useful to you than any other book about lawns. Why? The chapter heading above tells part of the reason, particularly the word regionalized. It means that no matter where in the South you live, Richmond, Fort Worth, Birmingham, or Miami, for example, there is something in this book for you.

The most extensive regional information is in the section, "Lawns in your area," beginning on page 80. These pages include the comments of lawn experts that live in each of the southern states. Who knows more about the finer points of lawn growing in Georgia, for instance, than an experienced individual living there?

Your climate is the single greatest factor to influence lawn growth. Climate determines whether Kentucky bluegrass or bermudagrass (or both) will thrive in your front yard. It dictates the right times to fertilize, water, and when crabgrass germinates. Diseases and weeds that are rampant in one climate are rare or nonexistent in another. It becomes easy to understand that climate is a very important reason why the information in this book is regionalized.

National lawn survey

To find out just what kind of information people wanted in a book on lawns, we conducted an extensive survey of lawn growers and nurserymen in every part of the country. They told us of the importance of knowing the "how and when" of lawn growing. "Be

regional and practical," they said. Their most common questions are discussed in the section, "Questions . . . questions . . . " beginning on page 4.

The lawn survey told us, to no great surprise, that people care about their lawns. Many homeowners projected an unabashed pride in being able to grow a handsome lawn. We discovered that, for most, the lawn is not just a hobby. Lawns are different things to different people — a soft playground for the kids, or a pleasant backdrop for the landscape. Maybe it's the soothing color or the uniform texture that induces a lawn's appeal. Whatever the attraction, a well-kept lawn does possess a certain mystique.

Many to thank

Without the Cooperative Extension Service offices of each state and their helpful workers, a book of this scope would not have been possible. For reference, we've listed their addresses beginning on page 80.

Without the help of acknowledged authorities, we could not guarantee our information as up-to-date and factual. Numerous individuals in the nursery, turf, and lawn maintenance business guided us toward the answers to everyday questions and problems that are commonplace to them.

To these many professionals, we express our appreciation.

You don't have to tell kids about the pleasures of going barefoot, especially when it comes to playing lawn games.

◁

There is nothing quite like an expanse of fresh green lawn — it's the perfect backdrop for summer daydreams.

Questions...questions

"Should I have my soil tested? If so, where?"

Soil testing reduces some of the guesswork involved in preparing a planting site. It's like any other project — eliminate possible problems before you start and success is more likely.

Most of the land grant colleges and universities will test soil samples for the residents of its state. Sometimes this is coordinated by the local Cooperative Extension Office. In states that don't offer soil testing programs, there are numerous private laboratories. Look for them in the yellow pages or ask your County Extension Agent for help.

Directions for taking a soil sample are on page 28. See also the addresses of state-provided soil testing beginning on page 80.

"Experts use the words straight, blend, and mixture when talking about lawn seed. What should I use?"

A *straight* is simply one type of seed of the same species and variety. An example is 'Adelphi' Kentucky bluegrass. Straights can be used for making your own mixture. Think twice, though, before planting an entire lawn with one kind of grass; disease or insect infestation can wipe it out.

A *blend* is two or more varieties of a single type of grass. A hypothetical blend of three Kentucky bluegrasses would combine 'Fylking,' 'Adelphi,' and 'Baron.' By blending, strengths are combined. A blend can produce quality, picture-perfect show lawns.

A *mixture* combines more than one species of grass per container. A typical mixture will have Kentucky bluegrass, fine fescue, and turf-type perennial ryegrass. A mixture is best for the average lawn. For most climates, they have the best insect and disease resistance, and overall adaptability.

"Should I buy seed or sod?"

Each has advantages and disadvantages. Improved varieties of cool-season grasses and warm-season grasses are frequently available as either seed or sod. A wider range of blends and mixtures is available as seed as compared to sod. St. Augustinegrass and the improved bermudagrasses are sold as sod, sprigs, or plugs and are not available as seed. Starting from seed is less expensive, but many home owners have trouble getting good establishment from a seeded lawn; the critical period of initial care is longer. Also, many weeds may start at the same time as the lawn seed. If your lawn seed was an inexpensive, low-quality mixture, weeds could possibly have been planted along with the seed (see pages 20 to 25), but more likely they were already in your soil.

Sod provides an instant lawn, is usually weed free, and of course germination is no problem. Sod can be a great help for starting a lawn on a slope (where seed can wash away), or for limited areas. For example, sod near an entryway will keep mud from being tracked inside the house.

"What type of grass should I buy?"

The best advice is, plant the grass that is well adapted in your area. Bermudagrass is an easy lawn grass to grow in most states in the South. Tall fescue makes a hardy lawn in transitional areas. Where the growing season is long, zoysiagrass will make a good, shade-tolerant lawn. Another shade-tolerant grass is St. Augustinegrass. Bahia and centipedegrass make low-maintenance lawns. Carpetgrass will thrive in wet, soggy soils. Kentucky bluegrass is often grown in the upper South, especially at higher elevations and inland. Mixed with turf-type ryegrass, it is more disease resistant.

One tip: Look around your neighborhood for the kind of lawn you like. If you find one that is appealing, ask the owner about it. Also, pages 9 to 19 have more extensive information on the grass varieties.

"Do I need to improve the soil if I buy sod?"

Soil preparation is the most important step in building any good lawn. Cultivate the soil as deep as possible (6 to 12 inches minimum), and add plenty of amendments (see page 27). Good soil promotes a healthy, deep rooted lawn that will need water less often. It will tend to be more resistant to attack by either disease or insects. In short, the better the soil before planting, the easier your lawn will be to take care of in the future. This is true whether you're starting a lawn from sod, seed, or any other way.

"How soon after seeding should I mow the lawn?"

Mow a new lawn for the first time after it has grown 30 to 40 percent higher than the regular mowing height. For example, a lawn to be maintained at 2 inches should be mowed when it reaches 2½ to 3 inches.

The mower blades should be sharp; the young grass plants can be easily pulled from the soil by a dull blade. The same thing happens if the lawn is mowed when it is too tall. Our staff favors either a manual push-reel mower or rotary mower for new lawns; they are lightweight and thus safer for new grass and less disturbing to soft soil.

New lawns from sprigs, stolons, plugs, or sod should be mowed with care the first time, but are established much sooner (especially sod) and don't need the delicate treatment required of a newly seeded lawn (see pages 48 to 51).

"How do I know when my lawn needs water?"

There are many ways to check for adequate water — visible signals, soil moisture meters, and coring tubes that actually let you see and feel the subsurface soil. Each is a guide and requires some experience and observation to employ.

Probably the simplest and most reliable signal is a change in turf color from bright green to a dull blue-green. This color change first occurs in the most drought-prone spots, especially beneath trees. Water as soon as it's noticed.

Another way of checking for water need is to take a walk across the lawn. Look to see if your footprint impressions remain visible for more than a few seconds. If the grass doesn't spring back fast, especially in the morning, water is needed.

"How often and how much should I water my lawn?"

To avoid wasteful overwatering, wait until the lawn shows signs of needing water (see preceding question). Then water thoroughly, enough to wet the soil down to the depth of the roots, usually about 6 to 8 inches. How often your lawn needs water will depend on your climate, soil, the time of year, the type of grass you have, how deeply rooted it is, and even how high you mow.

Wetting the soil to this 6 to 8-inch depth, assuming there is no run-off, will require about an inch of water in a loam soil, more if the soil is clay, and less if it is sandy. An inch of water over 1,000 square feet is about 625 gallons. A ½-inch diameter hose 50 feet long will deliver 350 gallons per hour (50 pounds of water pressure). Thus, it would take a little less than 2 hours to water 1,000 square feet.

"What type of mower should I buy?"

Power reel or rotary mowers are commonly used for home lawns. For either type, be certain the mowing height is adjustable to the height your lawn requires, and safety features are adequate. Older design rotaries do not have the important safety improvements of the new models. Push-reel types are the safest mowers.

The type of grass you have and the kind of lawn you want are very important considerations. Reel mowers, properly cared for, give the manicured, golf course look. They are *required* for low-growing grasses such as hybrid bermuda and bentgrass. Rotaries are better for taller growing, less intensively maintained lawns. They are also lighter weight, easier to handle than power reels, and less expensive, but they do require more frequent sharpening. See pages 48 to 51.

"How much fertilizer does my lawn need and when should I apply it?"

A lawn's need for fertilizer depends on the type of grass, the season, and the weather. Some grasses require much more than others for proper growth. Lawn experts talk in terms of "actual" nitrogen per 1,000 square feet. For instance, a 30-pound bag of 20% nitrogen (the first number of the analysis) has 6 pounds of actual nitrogen. Pages 11 to 15 tell about the individual grasses and how much nitrogen they need.

Spring and late summer to fall are the best times to fertilize cool-season grasses. Late spring is the best for warm-season grasses. Subsequent applications through spring and into summer are determined by the amount your lawn needs and the type of fertilizer you use. Fast release fertilizers should be used sparingly (usually no more than 1 pound of actual nitrogen per 1,000 square feet) and more frequently. Slow release types can be used more heavily (up to 2 or 3 pounds of actual nitrogen per 1,000 square feet) and less frequently. See pages 52 to 55 for more information on fertilizers.

"Should I remove clippings or let them filter down?"

There's no "yes" or "no" answer here. If your lawn is mowed often enough so that height is being reduced only one third or less, leaving the clippings should be no problem as long as they do not accumulate on the lawn surface. There are new types of mulching rotary mowers which help in dissipating clippings.

Clippings of cool-season grasses do not contribute significantly to thatch and do return some nutrients, permitting reduced fertilizer rates. But if there's a lot of clippings, they become unsightly and may suffocate grass trying to grow beneath. In such situations, removal of clippings is necessary.

"What is thatch?"

Thatch is the layer of grass stems, dead roots and debris that accumulates above the soil and below grass blades. The name thatch is well deserved. Like the thatched roof on a tropical hut, it stops water as well as fertilizer and most everything else from reaching the soil.

Thatch is not a problem until it becomes too thick. A thatched lawn will feel spongy underfoot. Insects and disease may develop in the thatch layer, and getting enough water and fertilizer into the soil becomes difficult.

Because of their horizontal or runner-type growth habit, St. Augustine, bermuda, and bentgrass are notorious thatch formers.

Zoysiagrass and fine fescue are wiry, tough, and slow to decompose, so they also tend to form thatch. On the other hand, perennial ryegrass rarely thatches badly. See pages 57 to 59 for ways to control thatch.

"How do I tell the difference between insect and disease damage?"

When you see a symptom such as a dead spot in your lawn, play the role of a "lawn doctor" — eliminate the most likely problems first. Spilled gasoline, fertilizer or chemical misuse, or even visits from the neighborhood dog can cause dead spots that look suspiciously like insect or disease damage.

Close examination of turf and soil will often reveal insects or where they have fed. Diseases may produce definite symptoms — spots, banding, discoloring. In many cases, grass that has died from disease is firmly attached to the ground (one exception is root and crown rot — the grass pulls up easily.) Grass killed by insect damage is often loosely attached.

Consider, also, the season. The disease that looks most like the offender may not be active at that time of year. The same is true of insects; some are at their worst in spring and fall, others in summer. See pages 60 to 79 for more on pest control.

"What can be done about broadleaf weeds like chickweed, clover, and black medic in my St. Augustinegrass lawn?"

Maybe you've already discovered the difficulty in ridding a lawn of these weeds. Technically, they're broadleaf and vining. They also have extensive root systems. Worse still, they are common in southern lawns.

First of all, plant quality seed or sod. Make sure it doesn't have too many weeds or weed seeds. If you're starting from plugs or sprigs, do a thorough job of soil preparation. This can include some kind of pre-plant weed control.

Your next line of defense is good lawn care. This means mowing at the right height and fertilizing and watering correctly. Good maintenance will go a long way in avoiding weed trouble. If your present lawn is overrun, there are weed controls specially designed for these and similar weeds in St. Augustine and other southern grasses like bahia, centipede, and bermuda. Use them in spring or fall when temperatures are low and weeds are actively growing.

"How do I know crabgrass when I see it? What can be done about it?"

Crabgrass is a weed well-known by name but little-known by sight. We've heard of it being confused with other weeds like tall fescue, timothy, and nimblewill.

Take a look at the weed photographs on pages 60 to 65. You can see how crabgrass differs from the stiffly upright, tall fescue. Crabgrass blades are wider and softer than timothy blades. Nimblewill forms dense patches and is perennial (lives through winter). Crabgrass thrives wherever summers are quite hot and particularly when very moist.

Crabgrass is an annual, meaning that it completes its entire life cycle in one season. It starts brand new from seed each spring, thus the key to its control. Use what's called a "pre-emergence" crabgrass killer. This product establishes a short-lived chemical barrier on the soil which kills crabgrass seedlings just as they begin to grow. Timing is important. There are ways to kill crabgrass once it has gained a foothold, but they are much more difficult.

"What is brown patch? Can I prevent it?"

Brown patch is really two things. One, it describes a symptom, a patch of dead grass. And two, it is the common name of a specific disease caused by the fungus *Rhizoctonia solani*. It can be confusing when the words "brown patch" are used to name both problems.

Literally, brown patch can be the result of a multitude of causes. Insects, fertilizer burn, or spilled gasoline are typical.

The fungus that causes brown patch is most damaging in transition zone areas during midsummer. Bentgrass can be severely damaged and, in the Southwest, St. Augustinegrass is often attacked. It's rare in cool summer areas such as the Pacific Northwest. Kentucky bluegrass is rarely bothered by the disease, ryegrass and fescue only moderately.

Brown patch disease is promoted by warm, humid weather. You can discourage it by fertilizing properly and by improving drainage of surface water. Several fungicides will prevent this disease. See pages 74 to 79.

Which grass?

This chapter is designed to help you select the grass that is right for you. Look for the one that best suits your climate, needs, and notions of what a lawn should be.

In the following pages we've described the 15 major grasses. Some grasses are naturally better adapted to specific climatic conditions. Each grass has an area where it is *best adapted,* but this should be considered a guide, and not absolute. Note the different recommendations for mowing and fertilization rates. These two differences are a tip-off to the high and low-maintenance grasses. The grasses that require short mowing and frequent, heavy fertilization are for dedicated lawn owners only.

Another difference in upkeep lies in the way grasses spread. For instance, bermuda and zoysiagrass spread from stems that run along the ground — beneath mower height. To keep these dense and smooth, it's important to mow short. These low-growers also tend to build up thatch rapidly.

New varieties rewrite lawn rules

The best of the improved Kentucky bluegrasses have dramatically increased disease resistance compared to common bluegrass types. Some tolerate lower mowing (to ¾ inch), compared to the 2 to 3 inches required for the older types. However, as grasses are cut lower, maintenance needs increase. The chart on page 16 describes the best Kentucky bluegrasses.

Probably the most significant breakthrough of recent years are the turf-type perennial ryegrasses. They are more persistent, more compatible

with Kentucky bluegrass and fine-fescue in both color and texture, and are cleaner mowing. (Common perennial rye has frayed tips that brown after mowing.)

Turf-type ryegrass has revolutionized seed mixtures, and is now a common component. They retain the ability to start fast like common perennial ryegrass, thus have been dubbed "crisis grass" by lawn professionals. Many of the turf-type ryegrasses are described on page 17.

The lawn business

Lawns are a big industry throughout this country, Canada, and Europe. A lot of the creeping red fescue seed planted around the world is grown in Canada. New varieties of bluegrass are being bred in Europe. Turfgrass research is carried on in several locations in this country. Tifton, Georgia, Texas A&M, Michigan State, Penn State, Rutgers University in New Jersey and areas in the Pacific

Northwest are just a few of the locations familiar to the experts. Most state and land grant colleges have at least one turf specialist on staff.

At the other end of the lawn care spectrum are the lawn service companies. These companies usually contract for specific jobs which the homeowner does not want to do himself, or perhaps does not know how to do, such as weed, disease and insect control, and renovation. Fertilization is often included in their programs. Some lawn companies provide their services on a once a year basis for special jobs while others will contract for year-around lawn care.

A lawn for your lifestyle

Of course, there can never be a perfect grass for every situation, that's why the decision as to what to plant is yours. But because of the work of the lawn experts, you can have a lawn *perfect for you.*

◁

Standing on a living patchwork of experimental grasses, Bill Meyer, turfgrass specialist, notes their performances.

The lawngrass you choose will have a great effect on the success of your lawn. Select a grass that is adapted to your area, and will match the type of use you expect it will receive. (Below: turfgrass test plot, Ohio State University.)

Grass climates

Below is our grass climate map. At best, all climate maps are generalities. Local conditions will vary by precipitation, temperature extremes, altitude, slope of the land, and soil types. These local characteristics, as well as maintenance practices, can play an important role in selecting a grass.

Grasses are categorized as either cool season, or warm season, according to their characteristics. Many warm-season grasses are adapted to the southern part of the United States. They grow vigorously in the warm summer months and then go dormant, turning brown with cold weather. Although better adapted to high temperatures, warm-season grasses usually aren't as hardy as cool-season grasses. Common warm-season types include bermuda, bahia, centipede, St. Augustine, and zoysiagrass. Buffalograss and blue grama are examples of warm-season grasses that can take colder climates.

Cool-season grasses are the grasses of the North. They grow actively in the cool weather of spring and fall, then grow slowly in summer heat but will remain green with ample water. Although they are primarily grown in the North, they are also valuable at higher elevations of the South.

In parts of the country with winter snow cover, active growth is in spring and fall. Kentucky bluegrass, fescue, bentgrass, and ryegrass are cool-season grasses.

Additional climate information can be found in "Lawns in your area," (see page 80). Beginning on page 11, the 15 most important lawn grasses are displayed. They are arranged in alphabetical order and each one is described in similar terms to make comparison easier.

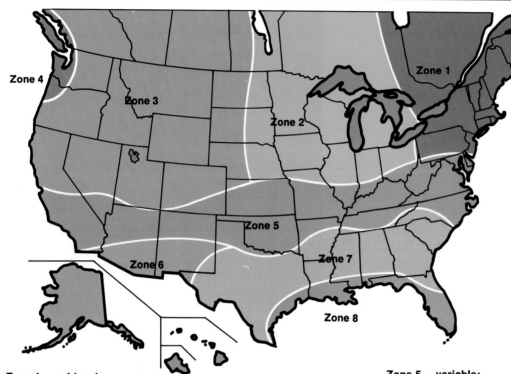

Zone 1 — cold and humid: This zone includes northeastern United States and southeastern Canada. It is an area of abundant rainfall and acid soils. Summers are hot and humid; winters are cold and snowy. Cool-season grasses such as Kentucky bluegrass, bentgrass, and fescue predominate. Zoysia and bermudagrass lawns are occasionally found in southern portions along the Atlantic Coast.

Zone 2 — cold winters and summer rains: Midwestern United States and central Canada make up this zone. Soils are not as acid and there is less rainfall compared to zone 1. Zone 2 is more acid than zone 3, but the winters are less cold. Summers are warm and humid, with frequent thunderstorms. With the exception of a few zoysiagrass lawns in the southern portion of this zone, cool-season grasses seem to predominate.

Zone 3 — cold and arid: This is a large and varied zone. It is comprized of the Great Plains States, including parts of Montana, South Dakota, North Dakota, Nebraska, and Wyoming. This area is subject to drying winds in both winter and summer with relatively little rain. Here, grasses are subject to the widest temperature fluctuation in the country. Aside from cool-season grasses, natives such as buffalograss and wheatgrass are utilized because of their drought tolerance and tenacity. The intermountain area supports fine fescues.

Zone 4 — cool and humid: This is the Pacific Northwest, west of the Cascade Range. Rain is plentiful and soils are typically acid. Lawns are cool-season grasses and stay a beautiful green all year. Compared to the Northeast, both summers and winters are milder.

Zone 5 — variable: This is a transition zone that runs across the entire United States. It is in in this zone that the grass climates overlap, depending on many local factors. Both warm-season and cool-season grasses are common. Selection of a proper grass type is critical, since neither cool-season nor warm-season grasses are ideally adapted in many areas. Tall fescue makes a good lawn in many areas of this zone. Good maintenance practices can make the difference between success and failure. Smart lawn owners pay close attention to the many different micro-climates around their homes.

Zone 6 — hot and dry summers: This zone is comprised of the arid Southwest, where rainfall is low and temperatures are high. All lawns here need some supplemental irrigation. Soils are usually alkaline. Lawns are primarily bermudagrass with some St. Augustine and zoysiagrass. In more northern areas, buffalograss and wheatgrass are sometimes used in low maintenance areas.

Zone 7 — hot and humid: Most lawns in this zone are made up of warm-season grasses such as bermuda, St. Augustine, and zoysiagrass. Rainfall is high and summers are warm and humid. Kentucky bluegrass may be useful in shady situations.

Zone 8 — tropical: This zone includes the Gulf Coast States, southern Florida, and much of Hawaii. Essentially a tropical climate, rainfall can be as high as 70 to 80 inches annually. Too much water is as much a problem here as too little water in the Southwest. In especially wet soils, carpetgrass is a good choice. Centipede, zoysia, bermuda, bahia, and St. Augustinegrass can make good lawns throughout this region.

A gallery of grasses

Bahiagrass

Strengths: Low maintenance. Extensive root system valued for erosion control and drought tolerance. Moderately aggressive.

Weaknesses: Forms a coarse, open lawn. Tall, fast-growing seed stalks need frequent mowing to remain attractive. Considered a weed in fine lawns. May turn yellow from chlorosis. Dollar spot and especially mole cricket may be a problem.

Shade tolerance: Fair to pretty good.

Water needs: Good drought resistance, but performs best where rain is plentiful and evenly distributed over the season.

Fertilizer needs. Medium, about 4 to 6 pounds of actual nitrogen per 1,000 square feet per year.

Wearability: Good.

Mowing height: High, to 3 inches.

Best adapted: Infertile, sandy soils. Central coast of North Carolina to east Texas. Popular in Florida.

Varieties: 'Argentine,' 'Pensacola.'

Scientific name: *Paspalum notatum*

Creeping bentgrass

Strengths: The grass of choice for golf course putting greens, lawn bowling, and similar uses. Can be mowed very low.

Weaknesses: Requires low mowing or else it quickly builds extensive thatch layer. Creeping bentgrass, like all bentgrasses, is susceptible to several diseases.

Shade tolerance: Somewhat tolerant, but best in full sun.

Water needs: High. Poor drought tolerance.

Fertilizer needs: Medium to high. Needs 6 to 10 pounds of actual nitrogen per 1,000 square feet per year for highest quality.

Wearability: Fair to good.

Mowing height: Keep it low, between ¼ and one inch.

Best adapted: Grows without special care in sandy-loam soils of northern U.S. and Canada. Extensively used in Pacific Northwest and Northeast.

Varieties: 'Penncross' is quick to establish, repairs itself fast. 'Penncross,' 'Emerald,' 'Seaside,' and 'Penneagle' start from seed. From sprigs: 'Cohansey,' 'Congressional,' and 'Toronto' creeping bentgrass.

Scientific name: *Agrostis palustris*

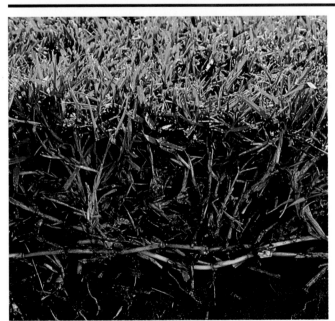

Bermudagrass
(manienie, devilgrass, wiregrass)

Strengths: Likes heat, easy to grow in most soils, takes considerable abuse. The most widely adapted warm-season grass. Tolerates little maintenance but makes a handsome lawn when given extra care.

Weaknesses: Invasive, poor shade tolerance, often browns in fall until spring.

Shade tolerance: Poor.

Water needs: Very drought tolerant but needs extra water in dry periods to look good.

Fertilizer needs: Moderate to high (4 to 8 lbs. per year per 1,000 square feet).

Wearability: Outstanding.

Mowing height: About 1 inch.

Best adapted: Lower elevations of the Southwest, Maryland to Florida in the east, then west to Kansas, Oklahoma, and Texas.

Varieties: Common.

Scientific name: *Cynodon dactylon*

Improved bermudagrass

Strengths: Most of the same virtues of common bermudagrass, but softer and finer textured. Generally shorter dormant season.

Weaknesses: More water, fertilizer, and mowing needed compared to common bermudagrass. Also more disease and insect prone. Requires regular thatch control.

Shade tolerance: Forget about growing it in the shade.

Water needs: Relatively drought tolerant but should get more than common bermudagrass.

Fertilizer needs: High: Up to 12 pounds or more of actual nitrogen per 1,000 square feet per year.

Wearability: Excellent.

Mowing height: ½ to 1 inch.

Best adapted: Very popular in the South and Southwest for a fine-quality lawn.

Varieties: (See chart, page 18).

Scientific name: *Cynodon* species

Common Kentucky bluegrass

Strengths: Not a good grass for the South (except at high elevations and northern transitional zones). With proper growing conditions, however, it looks the way many think a lawn is supposed to look — dark green, dense, with a medium texture.

Weaknesses: Disease prone. Suffers in summer heat.

Shade tolerance: Good shade lawn in upper South.

Water needs: Moderate to high.

Fertilizer needs: Medium. Between 4 to 6 pounds of actual nitrogen per 1,000 square feet per year.

Wearability: Poor in summer; okay in spring and fall.

Mowing height: 2 to 3 inches or higher.

Best adapted: Upper South, mountains, and piedmont.

Varieties: See page 16.

Scientific name: *Poa pratensis*

Improved Kentucky bluegrass

Strengths: As a group, color and density are superior to common Kentucky bluegrass. improved resistance to diseases such as leaf spot *(Helminthosporium)*, stripe smut *(Ustilago striiformis)*, and *fusarium* blight. Some varieties take heat better; some can be mowed shorter.

Weaknesses: Usually higher maintenance than common Kentucky bluegrass; more fertilizer is needed and more thatch build-up.

Shade tolerance: Improved in some varieties.

Water needs: Most varieties are more drought sensitive than common Kentucky bluegrass.

Fertilizer needs: Medium to high. About 4 to 8 pounds of actual nitrogen per 1,000 square feet per year. Some new varieties will do well on as little as 1 or 2 pounds of nitrogen per 1,000 square feet per year if established in good soil.

Wearability: Better than common Kentucky bluegrass.

Mowing height: Check the variety list on page 16.

Best adapted: Same as common Kentucky bluegrass.

Varieties: See page 16.

Scientific name: *Poa pratensis*

Centipedegrass

Strengths: Makes a good, low-maintenance, general purpose lawn. Adapts to poor soil. Aggressive enough to crowd out weeds. Needs less mowing than most grasses. Resistance to chinch bugs and rhizoctonia provides an alternative to St. Augustinegrass.

Weaknesses: Coarse textured. Color is not dark green. Tends to yellow from chlorosis. Sensitive to low temperatures.

Shade tolerance: Fair.

Water needs: Shallow root system is sensitive to drought but recovery is fast.

Fertilizer needs: Low, 3 pounds of actual nitrogen per 1,000 square feet per year.

Wearability: Not too good. Recovers slowly from damage.

Mowing height: To 2 inches.

Best adapted: Southern U.S. The northern limit would be a line drawn between northern Alabama and Raleigh, North Carolina.

Varieties: 'Centiseed' is a trade name for common centipede-grass that can be grown from seed. 'Oaklawn,' developed in Oklahoma, can be established by sprigs.

Scientific name: *Eremochloa ophiurides*

Dichondra

Strengths: Dichondra is not a grass, but a broadleaf plant. It makes a lush, dense, bright green carpet when well maintained. Needs less mowing than most grasses. Attacked by few diseases. Doesn't really have a bad season.

Weaknesses: Cutworms, flea beetles, snails and slugs prefer it to grass lawns. Hard to get weeds out once they invade.

Shade tolerance: Pretty good, better than bluegrass.

Water needs: High. Shallow root system cannot tolerate pro-longed drought.

Fertilizer needs: High. Likes frequent, light feeding of ½ to 1 pound of actual nitrogen per 1,000 square feet per month during growing season.

Wearability: Poor.

Mowing height: Depends on use. In shade where traffic is rare, mow a few inches high. Lower height to about one inch is best for most other lawn areas and helps keep out weeds.

Best adapted: Dichondra likes heat. Not adapted to cool, foggy climates or where temperatures drop below 25°F.

Varieties: None.

Scientific name: *Dichondra micrantha*

Chewing fescue

Strengths: Will tolerate close mowing in cool climate areas. Usually persistent in mixtures with Kentucky bluegrass.

Weaknesses: Same as red fescue. Competitiveness can be a disadvantage in mixtures with Kentucky bluegrass.

Shade tolerance: Same as red fescue.

Water needs: Low.

Fertilizer needs: Low. About 2 pounds of actual nitrogen per 1,000 square feet per year.

Wearability: Same as red fescue; may form clumps.

Mowing height: About 1 inch or higher.

Best adapted: Same as red fescue.

Varieties: See page 16.

Scientific name: *Festuca rubra commutata*

Red fescue, creeping red fescue

Strengths: Frequent component of bluegrass mixtures. Blends well and does what some bluegrasses can't do — grows well in shade or drought-dry soil. Fine texture, deep green color. Tolerates acid soil.

Weaknesses: Very susceptible to summer diseases in hot climates, especially in moist fertile soil.

Shade tolerance: Usually the best cool-season grass for dry shady lawns.

Water needs: Good drought tolerance.

Fertilizer needs: Low. 2 pounds at most per year.

Wearability: Poor. Slow to recover if damaged.

Mowing height: Normally, mow 2 inches or higher. After establishment it can be left unmowed for a "meadow look."

Best adapted: Where summers are cool such as coastal northwest, or at higher elevations.

Varieties: See page 17.

Scientific name: *Festuca rubra rubra*

Tall fescue

Strengths: A good, tough, play lawn. Some disease and insect resistance. Green all year. Good transition zone grass. Tall fescue is mostly used in shade too dense for St. Augustinegrass.

Weaknesses: Coarse textured, tends to clump. Not good in mixtures unless it comprises 80 or 90 percent of the mix. Must be seeded at a heavy rate.

Shade tolerance: Okay in partial shade.

Water needs: Good drought tolerance.

Fertilizer needs: Medium. Between 3 and 6 pounds of actual nitrogen per 1,000 square feet per year.

Wearability: Good in spring and fall when growth is fast. Less acceptable in summer.

Mowing height: Mow this one high — about 3 inches.

Best adapted: The best cool-season grass for transition areas. Takes heat.

Varieties: 'Kentucky 31.' 'Fawn' texture is less coarse. 'Alta' is wear resistant. 'Goars' most tolerant of poor soil. See chart, page 18.

Scientific name: *Festuca arundinacea*

Annual ryegrass
(Italian ryegrass, common ryegrass)

Strengths: Aggressive, fast germinating, quick to establish. Best use is overseeding in warm-winter areas.

Weaknesses: Poor cold and heat tolerance. Doesn't mow clean. Some perennial ryegrass seed is usually mixed with annual rye, which grows in weedy clumps.

Shade tolerance: Medium.

Water needs: High.

Fertilizer needs: Low to medium. Between 2 and 6 pounds of actual nitrogen per 1,000 square feet per year.

Wearability: Medium.

Mowing height: Around 1½ to 2 inches.

Best adapted: Same as perennial ryegrass. Use for overseeding dormant bermudagrass.

Varieties: None.

Scientific name: *Lolium multiflorum*

Turf-type perennial ryegrass

Strengths: Fast seed germination and establishment. Compatible in mixes with Kentucky bluegrass and fine fescues. Greater persistence than common perennial ryegrass. Cleaner mowing. Improved heat and cold tolerance. Tough play lawn.

Weaknesses: Suffers from winter kill in coldest climates. If it comprises more than 25 percent of a seed mix, it will impair establishment of the other grasses.

Shade tolerance: Medium.

Water needs: Intermediate.

Fertilizer needs: Medium. Apply between 3 and 6 pounds of actual nitrogen per 1,000 square feet per year.

Wearability: Fairly good.

Mowing height: 1 to 2 inches.

Best adapted: Coastal regions with mild winters and cool moist summers. Excellent for overseeding dormant bermudagrass in the South below adaptation line.

Varieties: See page 17.

Scientific name: *Lolium perenne*

St. Augustinegrass

Strengths: Easy to grow, robust. Good shade grass. Tolerates salty soil.

Weaknesses: Very susceptible to several diseases during prolonged rainy periods. Chinch bugs have killed many St. Augustinegrass lawns. In Texas, SAD virus (St. Augustinegrass Decline) has destroyed many lawns. Tends to thatch badly.

Shade tolerance: One of the best.

Water needs: Medium high; needs frequent watering.

Fertilizer needs: Give about 4 to 6 pounds of actual nitrogen per 1,000 square feet per year.

Wearability: Poor.

Mowing height: 1½ to 2½ inches.

Best adapted: Basically restricted to Gulf Coast states. St. Augustinegrass likes neutral to alkaline soils. Check for lime needs.

Varieties: 'Floratine' tolerates mowing to ½ inch and has a slightly more dense habit. 'Bitter Blue' has bluish color; is not wear tolerant. 'Floratam' is resistant to SAD virus, and tolerant of chinch bugs but is most cold sensitive.

Scientific name: *Stenotaphrum secundatum*

Zoysiagrass

Strengths: Forms dense, fine-textured lawn, resistant to weeds. Good heat and drought tolerance. Relatively free of disease and insect pests, though chinch bugs may bother it.

Weaknesses: Very slow to establish. Does not thrive where summers are too short or too cool. Wiry blades tough to mow if left too long. Tends to build thatch.

Shade tolerance: Slow in shade but much better than bermudagrass.

Water needs: Good but needs more than bermudagrass.

Fertilizer needs: Medium. Between 4 to 6 pounds of actual nitrogen per 1,000 square feet per year.

Wearability: Good.

Mowing height: ½ to 1½ inches.

Best adapted: Throughout the South. Occasionally used in the Northeast.

Varieties: 'Emerald' is a hybrid *(Zoysia japonica x Z. tenuifolia)* and probably the best (illustrated). *Zoysia japonica,* 'Meyer,' or 'Z-52' is much more coarse textured but more cold hardy. *Z. tenuifolia* is least cold tolerant but the finest textured.

Scientific name: *Zoysia* species

The variety charts

Varieties of Kentucky bluegrass

Variety	Description	Strengths	Comments
Adelphi	Very dark green with good density and medium texture.	Good summer performance and spring greenup; widely adapted.	Good resistance to leaf spot, stripe smut and *Fusarium* blight.
Baron	Dark green with medium texture and density.	Moderately good summer performance and widely adapted.	Moderately good resistance to leaf spot and stripe smut.
Bensun (A-34)	Light green with good density and fine texture.	Good shade performance and wear resistance. A very aggressive variety.	Good resistance to stripe smut and moderately good resistance to leaf spot.
Birka	Moderately dark green with good density and fine texture.	Moderately good shade performance.	Good resistance to leaf spot, stripe smut, powdery mildew.
Bonnieblue	Moderately dark green with medium texture and good density.	Good winter color and spring greenup.	Good resistance to leaf spot and stripe smut.
Bristol	Dark green with a medium coarse texture and good density.	Moderately good shade tolerance.	Good resistance to leaf spot, stripe smut and powdery mildew.
Columbia	Moderately dark green with good density and fine texture.	Good winter color and spring greenup; moderately good heat tolerance.	Good resistance to leaf spot, stripe smut and *Fusarium* blight.
Delta	Medium green with an upright growth habit and moderate density.	Moderate drought tolerance.	Very susceptible to leaf spot. Prone to chlorosis in alkaline soils.
Fylking	Moderately dark green with fine texture.	Good sod former.	Good resistance to leaf spot, moderately resistant to stripe smut but susceptible to *Fusarium* blight. Best kept mowed 1½ inches or lower.
Glade	Dark green with very good density and fine texture.	Moderately good shade tolerance.	Moderately good resistance to leaf spot and good resistance to stripe smut and powdery mildew.
Kenblue	Medium green with an upright growth habit and moderate density.	Best at low maintenance levels — high cutting and low fertility.	Susceptible to leaf spot.
Majestic	Dark green with a medium texture and good density.	Good winter color and spring greenup.	Good resistance to leaf spot; moderately good resistance to stripe smut.
Merion	Dark green with a medium coarse texture with good density.	Good heat and drought tolerance and transplanting ability in the heat.	Good resistance to leaf spot; susceptible to stripe smut, powdery mildew, and rust. Not good in the shade.
Newport	Moderately dark green with medium texture and density.	Good winter color.	Susceptible to leaf spot and *Fusarium*.
Nugget	Dark green with very fine texture and high density; poor color in winter.	Very good cold hardiness.	Good resistance to leaf spot and powdery mildew; susceptible to dollar spot.
Parade	Medium green with good density and fine texture.	Good winter color and spring greenup.	Good resistance to leaf spot, stripe smut, and *Fusarium* blight.
Park	Moderately dark green with an upright growth habit and moderate density.	Best performance at low maintenance levels which includes high cutting and low fertility.	Susceptible to leaf spot and *Fusarium* blight. Prone to yellowing in alkaline soils.
Sydsport	Medium green with good density and medium texture.	Good sod former; wear tolerant, widely adapted.	Moderately good leaf spot, stripe smut, and powdery mildew resistance.
Touchdown	Moderate dark green with very good density and fine texture.	Moderately good tolerance of low mowing and shade; good winter color and spring greenup.	Good resistance to leaf spot, stripe smut, and powdery mildew.
Victa	Dark green with medium texture and density.	Moderately good summer performance; widely adapted.	Moderately good resistance to leaf spot and stripe smut.
Warrens A-20	Dark green with a medium texture and good density.	Good spring greenup.	Good resistance to leaf spot and stripe smut.
Windsor	Moderately dark green with moderately good density and texture.	Good spring greenup.	Susceptible to stripe smut; moderately resistant to leaf spot.

Varieties of turf-type perennial ryegrass

Variety	Description	Strengths	Comments
Birdie	Medium green with good density and fine texture.	Good heat tolerance.	Good resistance to brown patch; moderate resistance to crown rust. Good mowing qualities with stemming period in the spring.
Citation	Dark green with good density and fine texture.	Good heat tolerance.	Good resistance to brown patch; moderate resistance to red thread. Good mowing qualities. Stemming period in the spring.
Derby	Moderately dark green. Good density and texture.	Moderately good heat and cold tolerance.	Good resistance to brown patch; good mowing qualities.
Diplomat	Moderately dark green; very good density and fine texture.	Moderately good heat and cold tolerance.	Good resistance to brown patch; good mowing qualities.
Loretta	Light green with very good density and fine texture.	Moderately good cold tolerance and very good mowing qualities.	Good resistance to crown rust; no stemming period in spring and lower performance in the summer.
Manhattan	Medium green with good density and fine texture.	Good cold tolerance and good performance in the spring and fall.	Moderately good resistance to brown blight; good mowing qualities and no stemming period.
NK-200	Moderately dark green with moderately good density and texture.	Good cold tolerance.	Moderately good resistance to *Fusarium* patch.
Norlea	Dark green; intermediate density and texture.	Good cold tolerance.	Moderately good resistance to *Fusarium* patch. Mowing quality less desirable than other varieties. Susceptible to crown rust.
Omega	Moderately dark green with good density and texture.	Moderately good heat and cold tolerance.	Good resistance to brown blight and moderate resistance to brown patch. Good mowing qualities with short stemming period.
Pennfine	Moderately dark green with good density and texture.	Good heat tolerance.	Good resistance to brown patch and moderately good resistance to brown patch. Good mowing qualities with stemming period in the spring.
Regal	Dark green with moderately good density and texture.	Moderately good heat tolerance.	Moderately good brown patch resistance. Moderately good mowing qualities.
Yorktown I	Dark green with good density and texture.	Moderately good heat and cold tolerance.	Moderately good brown patch and brown blight resistance. Good mowing qualities.
Yorktown II	Dark green with very good density and fine texture.	Moderately good heat and cold tolerance.	Good resistance to brown patch and crown rust; very good mowing qualities.

Varieties of fine fescues

Variety	Description	Strengths	Comments
Banner	Chewings type, dark green, good density and fine texture.	Moderately good disease resistance and tolerant of close mowing.	Very competitive with Kentucky bluegrasses in mixtures. Susceptible to powdery mildew.
Boreal	Creeping type, moderately dark green. Medium texture and density.	Good seedling vigor.	Has good winter hardiness.
Cascade	Chewings type. Medium green with very fine texture.	Good establishment rate.	Susceptible to leaf spot.
C-26	Hard fescue type, dark green, fine texture, and good density.	Good disease resistance compared to the other fine fescues. Good drought tolerance.	Should perform well in mixtures with Kentucky bluegrass.
Dawson	Semi-creeping type, medium green, good density and fine texture.	Moderately good leaf spot resistance and tolerant of close mowing. Good for overseeding bermudagrass.	Can be damaged severely by dollar spot.
Fortress	Creeping type forming extensive rhizomes. Dark green with medium texture and density.	Good resistance to powdery mildew and good seedling vigor.	Blends well with Kentucky bluegrasses and recovers well from summer injury.
Highlight	Chewings type. Medium green with fine texture and good density.	Moderately good disease resistance and tolerant of close mowing.	Very competitive with Kentucky bluegrass in mixtures.

(Chart continued on page 18)

Varieties of fine fescues, continued

Variety	Description	Strengths	Comments
Illahee	Creeping type. Dark green, medium texture and density.	Good seedling vigor.	Blends well with Kentucky bluegrasses.
Jamestown	Chewings type. Dark green, good density and fine texture.	Moderately good disease resistance and tolerant of close mowing.	Very competitive with Kentucky bluegrass in mixtures. Susceptible to powdery mildew.
Pennlawn	Predominantly a creeping type. Medium dark green, good density and fine texture.	A widely adapted variety with moderate disease resistance.	Used widely in mixtures with Kentucky bluegrasses.
Ruby	Creeping type. Dark green, medium texture and density.	Good seedling vigor.	Blends well with Kentucky bluegrasses.
Wintergreen	Chewings type. Moderately dark green, fine texture and good density.	Good winter color and rust resistance.	Good winter hardiness, used in northern areas.

Varieties of tall fescue

Variety	Description	Strengths	Comments
Alta	Upright growing and coarse texture. Medium green.	Drought tolerant. Moderately persistent in turf.	Has performed equal to Kentucky 31 in Northern California.
Fawn	Upright growing and coarse texture. Medium green.	Drought tolerant.	Susceptible to crown rust. Not as persistent in turf as Alta and Kentucky 31.
Goar	Upright growing and coarse texture. Medium green.	Drought tolerant.	Lacking competitive ability compared to Alta and Kentucky 31.
Kentucky 31	Coarse texture and somewhat lower growing than Alta and Fawn. Medium green.	Drought tolerant. Widely adapted to many soil types. Moderately disease resistant.	Good persistence in turf in transition zone. Good winter recovery and spring green up.
Kenwell	Slightly lower growing than Kentucky 31 with coarse texture. Medium green.	Drought tolerant. Better fall color than Kentucky 31 in fall.	Similar to Kentucky 31 with slightly better disease resistance.

Varieties of bermudagrass

Variety	Description	Strengths	Comments
Midiron	Medium texture, dark green.	Most winter hardy of the bermudagrasses. Best tolerance to winter traffic. Vigorous, fast rate of coverage.	Used primarily in upper South and transition zone for tees and fairways. Also used on athletic fields.
Midiron-Tifway Blend	Medium texture, dark green.	Combines vigor and winter hardiness with frost resistance and dense growth for wear resistance and longer period of color retention.	Used on tees, fairways, and athletic fields in the upper South.
Ormond	Medium fine texture, blue-green.	Vigorous, rapid spreading and wear tolerant. Doesn't tend to thatch as much as other bermudagrasses. Is subject to winterkill, mites and diseases.	Used mostly in Florida for golf-course fairways, athletic fields, and home lawns.
Tifdwarf	Fine texture, dark green.	Tolerates consistent low mowing down to ⅛ inch.	Used primarily on golf greens and home lawns.
Tifgreen	Fine texture, medium green.	Tolerates close mowing and heals rapidly.	Most popular grass for putting greens in the southeast. Also used on home lawns and grass tennis courts.
Tiflawn	Medium fine texture, bright green.	Accepts a lot of traffic, fast recovery from wear. Performs reasonably well under low maintenance. Good tolerance to herbicides.	Used primarily for athletic fields. Is subject to winterkill in upper South.
Tifway	Fine texture, dark green.	Forms a dense, weed-resistant turf. Frost tolerant; withstands a lot of wear. Overall, less maintenance requirements than other bermudagrasses. Good tolerance to herbicides.	Most popular tee and fairway grass in the southeast. Most popular grass for athletic fields, as well as the most popular bermudagrass for home lawns. In the upper South, is subject to winterkill.

The improved bermudagrasses of the Tif series were developed or discovered and released through the University of Georgia's Coastal Plains Experiment Station and the U.S.D.A. In contrast to common bermudagrass, the Tif varieties are more disease resistant, have greater density, better weed resistance, fewer seed heads, and finer, softer textures with better color. They are especially well suited to playgrounds, football fields, and golf courses.

Lawngrass comparisons

The following lists compare the specific types of grass in general terms. They are based on the personal observations of many specialists, and are not absolute. The specific qualities of one grass could vary, and newly developed varieties may enter at different positions in the lists.

A particular grass type may seem perfect for your home lawn. However, there are many other factors you should take into consideration, such as adaptation to your climate and maintenance requirements. For instance, where warm-season grasses are best adapted, the cool-season grasses naturally drop out of the lists and vice versa.

High temperature tolerance

Tolerant / **Intolerant**

zoysiagrass
improved bermudagrass
common bermudagrass
St. Augustinegrass
paspalum
carpetgrass
centipedegrass
bahiagrass
buffalograss
tall fescue
dichondra
Kentucky bluegrass
perennial ryegrass
creeping bentgrass
colonial bentgrass

High temperature tolerance depends on variety and maintenance practices, and a whole range of climatic factors that affect growth habits. Raising the cutting height of a cool-season grass will improve its temperature tolerance. Also, only tolerance to high temperatures is more pronounced in transitional areas, since the grass is not as well adapted.

Accepts low mowing

Best / **Worst**

creeping bentgrass (¼ inch or less)
improved bermudagrass
colonial bentgrass
common bermudagrass
zoysiagrass
buffalograss
carpetgrass
centipedegrass
paspalum
red fescue
perennial ryegrass
Kentucky bluegrass
St. Augustinegrass
tall fescue
bahiagrass

Mowing height is primarily determined by the growth habit of the grass. Those that spread horizontally can be clipped lower. There are certain cool-season varieties such as 'Merion' Kentucky bluegrass that can be cut at ¼ inch to ⅜ inch for backyard putting greens, but this is seldom recommended. In general, Kentucky bluegrass cut above 1½ inches is much easier to keep.

Drought tolerance

Very high / **Not at all**

bahiagrass
zoysiagrass
buffalograss
common bermudagrass
improved bermudagrass
tall fescue
red fescue
carpetgrass
centipedegrass
paspalum
St. Augustinegrass
colonial bentgrass
dichondra
creeping bentgrass
Kentucky bluegrass
perennial ryegrass

A grass may tend to remain green and resist short periods of drought. However, this same grass may, if subjected to severe drought, die out completely.

Requires the least fertilizer

A little / **A lot**

buffalograss
red fescue
centipedegrass
carpetgrass
bahiagrass
tall fescue
perennial ryegrass
Kentucky bluegrass
zoysiagrass
St. Augustinegrass
paspalum
common bermudagrass
improved bermudagrass
dichondra
colonial bentgrass
creeping bentgrass

While a lawn may exist on rather low amounts of fertilizer, high or desirable quality may only come with increased amounts. The variety, type, and climate greatly influence fertilizer needs.

Disease resistant

Best / **Worst**

zoysiagrass
buffalograss
bahiagrass
carpetgrass
centipedegrass
improved bermudagrass
common bermudagrass
St. Augustinegrass
tall fescue
paspalum
red fescue
Kentucky bluegrass
dichondra
perennial ryegrass
colonial bentgrass
creeping bentgrass

A grass may be indicated as having few disease problems, but this chart represents composite knowledge of the overall disease situation. Under the right environmental conditions, a single disease may be quite devastating, for example, brown patch on St. Augustinegrass.

Shade tolerance

Tolerant / **Intolerant**

red fescue
tall fescue
St. Augustinegrass
dichondra
colonial bentgrass
creeping bentgrass
paspalum
bahiagrass
carpetgrass
centipedegrass
perennial ryegrass
Kentucky bluegrass
zoysiagrass
buffalograss
improved bermudagrass
common bermudagrass

Shade tolerance of a turf depends upon many conditions. If the site is quite damp, roughstalk bluegrass could persist, while red fescue would die out completely. On a dry site, it would be the opposite. Often there are also significant varietal differences.

Establishment time from seeds or stolons

Fast / **Slow**

improved bermudagrass (stolons)
common bermudagrass
perennial ryegrass
creeping bentgrass (stolons)
St. Augustinegrass
paspalum
carpetgrass
bahiagrass
centipedegrass
tall fescue
bentgrass (seed)
buffalograss
red fescue
Kentucky bluegrass
dichondra
'Emerald' zoysiagrass

The point at which a new planting becomes a lawn depends upon the lawn owner. If the lawn is only to keep the soil in place, a new seeding (at a heavy rate) of perennial ryegrass or tall fescue can do the job in as little as 2 to 3 weeks.

Wearability

High / **Low**

zoysiagrass
improved bermudagrass
bahiagrass
common bermudagrass
buffalograss
tall fescue
Kentucky bluegrass
carpetgrass
perennial ryegrass
red fescue
St. Augustinegrass
centipedegrass
paspalum
colonial bentgrass
creeping bentgrass
dichondra

In many situations, traffic is much more than any turfgrass can tolerate. Again, there is a lot of varietal variability. 'Bensun,' 'Baron,' and 'Merion' Kentucky bluegrass take traffic rather well.

Lawn seed – from the ground up

Seed is the most common way to start a new lawn. Years ago, what was swept from the barn could be scattered around the yard and eventually, a lawn would grow. This casual and haphazard approach has been superceded by a very sophisticated industry that supplies around 120 million pounds of lawn seed to grow turf each year.

Of the millions of pounds of seed produced, Kentucky bluegrass is the most important. It is the most widely adapted grass of North America. Common bermudagrass is also planted in large quantities, with fine and tall fescue and the ryegrasses being the other important lawn seeds.

Seed is a popular method to start lawns, partly because it's economical. Computing the total expense of a new lawn, the seed is usually no more than five percent of the total cost.

Seed quality is important. Quality seed is healthy, with a high percentage of germination. It is also weed and disease free. A few more dollars for five pounds of the highest possible quality seed for example, can save hundreds of dollars in the years ahead. You'll have fewer weed and disease problems and will generally have a higher quality lawn.

The keys to starting with seed

Experience has shown that the type of seed you select is very important. Make sure the grass type and variety are adapted to your area. Read the label on the seed container carefully. Prepare the soil well and ensure good contact between the seed and the soil when planting. Sow the seed at the time of year most favorable to germination (see pages 27 to 31). Keep the new seed bed moist until after germination. Be certain you have the answers to these important questions before you purchase the seed.

☐ Will your lawn be used primarily for decoration or for recreation?

☐ Which grasses are best adapted to where you live?

☐ Will the lawn be partially shaded or receive full exposure to the sun?

☐ How much time and energy are you willing to put into lawn care?

These questions may seem obvious, but they are very important considerations. Most can be answered by referring to the descriptions of the grasses on the previous pages.

Good seed doesn't cost, it pays

Although some aspects of lawn seed production are under state and federal regulations, the seed producers desire for quality is the only sure guarantee of good seed. But by knowing how to read a seed label, many comparisons can be made that will help you make a better decision.

The variety of boxes and containers of lawn seed available in most garden centers and hardware stores can make selecting lawn seed a bewildering experience. Besides the color and size of the box and a brand name, there is no way to compare value other than reading the label.

Seed box labeling is government regulated. The Federal Seed Act of 1939 determines the basic structure of seed labels. Many individual states have their own seed labeling laws but any variance from the federal standard is usually insignificant.

There is no real mystery to seed labels, but because of government regulations and the use of a technical vocabulary, they can be difficult for the casual or beginning gardener to understand. Seed labels are a legal document; each word has a specific meaning.

The sample seed label illustrated on the opposite page shows and briefly explains the major parts of a typical label. The following is a more detailed account.

Understanding a seed label

Directions for use: Most commercial mixes will tell you how much seed to use and sometimes when to seed. Some will indicate the spreader setting to use.

The spreader setting is merely a guide, although usually an adequate one. A statement like "enough seed for 1,000 square feet of new lawn," is better. You then know how far the seed will go, regardless of how you intend to spread it.

Experts have determined how many seeds per square inch are best for new seedings. These rates will vary according to many factors, such as the seed size and the growth habit of the grass. But most lawns get a good start if seeded at a rate of approximately 20 seeds per square inch — just less than 3 million seeds per 1,000 square feet. (These figures certainly are not intended to be precise and only serve as an example.) Some quick multiplication will show that 3 million seeds per 1,000 square feet is the same as 1 pound of Kentucky bluegrass per 1,000 square feet or 5 pounds of fine fescue over that same area. For more on this, take a look at "Seed facts" on page 23.

It is interesting to note that different varieties of the same type of grass will vary in seed size. However, the difference is inconsequential when determining application rates. For example, 'Sydsport' Kentucky bluegrass has 1,800,000 seeds per pound, while 'Birka' has only 1,380,000 seeds per pound.

To recreate the "shades of shade" found around the home, shade cloths of varying densities are placed above test grasses. Turf researchers then record the respective tolerances.

Naturally, the quantity recommended to sow is based on average conditions. If you expect a lot of the seeds to be eaten by birds, or otherwise fail to survive past germination, sow at a heavier rate. But seeding heavily just to be generous is not always a good idea. Grasses planted too closely together will produce weaker plants that are slower to mature.

"Fine-textured" and "Coarse": The fine-textured grasses are the backbone of a high quality lawn seed mix. Kentucky bluegrass and the fine fescues are the most important fine-textured types.

Bentgrasses are also considered fine-textured. At one time, they were a component of all quality mixes. They are soft and their narrow leaf-blades qualify them as fine textured, but because of their different growth habit and management needs, they do not mix well with Kentucky bluegrass, fine fescue, or turf-type perennial ryegrass. They form unattractive clumps in a bluegrass lawn if the lawn is mowed high. Mowed low, the bentgrass will eventually predominate anyway because the others will be crowded out. Alone and properly cared for, the bentgrasses can make a handsome lawn.

Bluegrasses other than Kentucky types *(Poa pratensis)* are also legally considered fine-textured. Rough-stalk bluegrass *(P. trivialis)* is found in some shady lawn mixes. Bermudagrass is also listed as fine-textured. All other grasses must, by law, be listed as "Coarse."

Specifically, the coarse grasses are tall fescue, meadow fescue, redtop, timothy, and both annual and perennial ryegrass. However, considering the ryegrasses in this category is a bit problematical. It is true that annual and common perennial ryegrasses are wide bladed, clump forming, coarse grasses. But the new varieties of perennial ryegrass, called "turf types," are as fine-bladed as Kentucky bluegrass. These turf-type ryes are premium quality lawngrasses, some labeled as fine-textured, others unfairly labeled as coarse. Thus, it is

Reading a seed label

This label is an example of what you will find on the shelf at your garden store. The proportions of the actual grasses listed are only a sample. The low percentages of weed and crop seed, the absence of noxious weeds, and the high germination percentages indicate a high quality mixture.

These are the backbone of quality lawns, the common high-quality grasses, such as Kentucky bluegrass and fine fescue.

Where the seed crop was grown must be shown for seed quantities greater than 5% of the mixture. This has no bearing on adaptation of the grass.

This is the quality most subject to change, for the worse, as the seed ages. It represents the percent of viable seed that will germinate under ideal conditions. This varies with the grass.

Look for named varieties. They're considered superior to common types, and in most cases are a sign of quality.

This percentage is the proportion of the grass by weight, not seed count. See "Seed facts" page 23.

Generally, "coarse kinds" tend to clump and don't mix well with other grasses. If there are any listed, they should not total more than 50% (One exception are the turf-type ryegrasses. By law, some are listed as coarse, but they are actually fine-textured.)

It's virtually impossible to keep all weed seeds out of a crop, but look for less than 1 percent. Weeds included here are regulated by state law.

These are seeds of any commercially grown crop. They may be other turfgrasses, or real problems, like timothy or orchardgrass. Look for "zero crop seed" or as close as possible.

All the chaff, dirt, and miscellaneous that manages to escape cleaning is inert matter. It's harmless, but shouldn't total more than 3 or 4 percent.

Noxious weeds are the most troublesome. In most states, it is illegal to sell seed that contains certain noxious weeds. They must be individually named and the number of seeds per ounce indicated. Quality seed should have none.

This is the guarantee of other information, particularly percent germination. Current dates are best, but seed stored in a cool, dry place will last months longer.

Fine-textured Grasses	Origin	Germination
30% Kentucky bluegrass	Oregon	80%
20% Merion Kentucky bluegrass	Oregon	80%
20% Fylking Kentucky bluegrass	Oregon	80%
30% Creeping red fescue	Canada	90%
Coarse Kinds	**Other Ingredients**	
None claimed	0.01% Crop seed 1.05% Inert matter 0.03% Weed seed No noxious weeds Tested: Within 9 months of today's date.	

Germination percentages let you know how many of each seed type will germinate under ideal conditions as of the test date. By multiplying the percent germination and the percent of the grass type in the mixture, you can determine how many seeds of that type have the potential to grow. This is called "percent-pure live seed." This percentage is not listed on the label, but it's one way, although complicated, to figure the real value of the seed before purchase.

Let's go back to our sample of 60% bluegrass and 40% fine fescue mixture. If the germination percentage of the bluegrass is 80%, then 60% multiplied by 80% (.60 x .80) equals the percent-pure live seed of Kentucky bluegrass. Usually 90% of the fine fescue will germinate. So, 90% multiplied by 40% equals the pure live seed of fescue in the mixture. In these terms the mixture is actually 48% Kentucky bluegrass and 36% red fescue. Obviously, as the germination percentage goes down, you are buying less viable seed.

If a container of seed is unmixed and unblended, it will list the percent "purity." Essentially, this has the same meaning as the percentage of grass types in a seed mixture mentioned earlier. A box of straight Kentucky bluegrass should be at least 90% pure. Again, by multiplying the percent purity by the germination percentage, you can determine how many viable seeds are in the box, thus the value of the seed.

Percent-pure live seed is a good way to compare value but is not the

Rust disease can be devastating to seed growers; naturally resistant varieties are valued.

apparent that the term coarse can be misleading, and can cause problems. If you know something about the seed in the box and its potential, you can be the best judge.

Percentages: When the label says that 60% of a given mixture is Kentucky bluegrass and 40% is red fescue, it means 60% and 40% by *weight* of the contents. If the meaning of this is not apparent, take a look at "Seed facts." Note that there are usually over 2 million seeds of

Kentucky bluegrass in a pound, and approximately 600,000 seeds per pound of red fescue. When you plant a mixture labeled as 60% Kentucky bluegrass and 40% red fescue, in actual seed numbers you are planting 84% bluegrass and 16% red fescue. A red fescue seed weighs three times more than a seed of Kentucky bluegrass. The actual contents of a seed mixture would be more apparent if the percentages were in seed counts, rather than weight.

Here's how a breeder makes a quick field check of a grasses' seed production. The seed heads are removed from the plant (left), and gently rubbed between the palms (center). The seed easily separates from the hulls (right).

only measure. In terms of the label, judge quality primarily by comparing percent germination, percent weed and crop seed, and the occurrence, if any, of noxious weeds.

"Crop" and "Weed" seed: Plants that are considered crop and those considered weeds are distinguished by agricultural laws of individual states. Keep in mind that labeling laws were designed for farmers, not buyers of lawn seed. That's why some of the most serious lawn weeds may not be listed under "Weeds." Timothy, orchardgrass, tall fescue, and brome-grass — all serious lawn weeds — are usually classified as crop. Just 1% of a weedy fescue can contribute 10,000 seeds to every 1,000 square feet of new lawn. Both timothy and redtop have small vigorous seeds. A small percentage of these can produce many established weeds in the new lawn.

Consider likewise, the percentage of weed seeds. The percent could represent a few large, harmless weeds, or many serious lightweight weed seeds. The quality of the producer is the only standard to judge by. At a 0.27% weed percentage, for instance, a homeowner can plant 30 unwanted chickweed seeds per square foot.

"Noxious" weeds: These weeds are often difficult to eliminate once they're established. Many spread just as aggressively with runners or bulbs as by seed. Each state will have a list of weeds considered noxious.

The specific noxious weeds as set forth by the Federal Seed Act are: whitetop (*Lepidium draba, Lepidium repens, Hymenosphysa pubescens*); Canada thistle (*Cirsium arvense*); dodder (*Cuscuta* sp.); quackgrass (*Agropyron repens*); johnsongrass (*Sorghum halepense*); bindweed (*Convoulus arvensis*); Russian knap-weed (*Centaurea picris*); perennial sowthistle (*Sonchus arvensis*); and leafy spurge (*Euphorbia esula*). These are primarily field crop weeds, but a few are serious lawn weeds.

Annual bluegrass (*Poa annua*) and bermudagrass are noxious weeds in a few states. If present in a seed mix-ture, noxious weeds must be named and the number of seeds per ounce shown. In a quality seed mixture, there should be none.

Straights, mixes, and blends
The word "straight" is used to de-scribe lawn seed composed of just one type of grass. Many warm-

Seed facts

Name	Use	No. seeds per lb.	Lbs. seed per 1,000 sq. ft.	% purity	% germi-nation	Days to germinate*
Bahiagrass	Low maintenance. Gulf Coast.	175,000	8	75	70	21-28
Bentgrass, creeping	Putting/bowling greens. Cool moist climates.	6,500,000	1	98	90	4-12
Bermuda, common	Good play lawn. Most important grass of southern states.	1,750,000	2	97	85	7-30
Blue grama	Low maintenance, drought tolerant. Northern Plains.	800,000	2	40	70	15-30
Bluegrass, Kentucky	Widely adapted, all-purpose.	2,200,000	2	90	80	6-30
Buffalo-grass	Central Plains, tough, drought tolerant, low maintenance.	290,000	5	85	—	20-30
Carpetgrass	Tropical, wet soils, low maintenance.	1,300,000	2	—	90	21
Centipede-grass	Gulf Coast, low maintenance.	410,000	½	50	70	14-20
Dichondra	Southwest. Lawnlike ground cover.	—	2	99.5	75	14-24
Fescue, fine	Widely adapted. Tolerant of shade. Takes dry soil.	615,000	5	97	90	5-10
Fescue, tall	Good transition zone grass. Tough play lawn. Use by itself.	230,000	12	97	90	7-12
Ryegrass, annual	Quick cover for winter overseeding.	230,000	9	97	90	3-7
Ryegrass, perennial	Improved types called "crisis grass." Good in mixes. Common kinds coarse and clumpy.	230,000	9	97	90	3-7

*Varies according to growing conditions

season lawns are unmixed and un-blended with other grass types. Lawns of common or improved bermuda, St. Augustine, or zoysiagrass are examples. Tall fescue and bentgrass are cool-season grasses that are sometimes used alone. For most cool-season lawns, a mixture or blend is preferred.

A mixture contains different vari-eties of seed which adjust individually to the varying soil conditions and sun or shade areas of typical lawns. The strength of one grass type compen-sates for another's weakness. A lawn of a single variety of Kentucky blue-grass could be wiped out if a potent disease swept through. With consider-able amounts of fescue or rye in the lawn, the effect of the disease is lessened.

In the past, a little bit of everything was thrown into a bag of lawn seed. It was the shotgun approach — grow-

ers weren't too sure what was going to work so a little of everything was tried.

Also, some still speak of the "nurse-grass" in a mixture. The idea of a nursegrass, disregarded today, is that a hardy, fast-growing grass makes the way a little easier for the slower, more delicate premium grass. We now know the fast grasses actually compete too much with the others and slow estab-lishment of the premium grass.

The grasses that mix together best will have similar color, texture, and growth rate. They will be roughly equal in aggressiveness. The most important grasses that are similar in these respects are Kentucky blue-grass, fine fescue, and the turf-type ryegrasses. Seed formulators vary the relative amounts of these ingredients and sometimes add small amounts of other grasses, depending upon the intended use of the mixture. For in-stance, more fescue will be added if the lawn will be partly shaded or if the soil is drought prone. More turf-type ryegrass will get the lawn off to a fast start. More Kentucky bluegrass will produce the show lawn. Opinions of many experts and regional considerations also play an important part in making up a seed mixture.

Many good packaged lawn seeds are a combination of a mixture and a blend. A blend is a combination of varieties from one species. Characteristically, a blend is between a regular mixture and a straight. Resistance to particular diseases are somewhat improved and there is a look of consistency in texture and color. Seed containers that announce something like "an all-bluegrass mixture" are technically blends.

Measures of extra-quality seed

Almost every state has a program of seed certification. Technically, "certified" seed only guarantees varietal purity. In other words, if the label says "Certified 'Adelphi' Kentucky bluegrass," the contents of the bag are guaranteed to be 'Adelphi' Kentucky bluegrass.

In most states certified seed also ensures higher overall quality. Fewer weed seeds and other crop contaminates, as well as less inert filler are also guaranteed.

"Percent fluorescence" is a special rating of perennial ryegrass. The photographs on this page show what fluorescing seed looks like. In 1929, it was discovered that annual ryegrass secreted a fluorescent substance when it was germinated on white filter paper. By contrast, the improved, turf-type ryes secrete none of this substance.

A simple way to test for contamination of improved ryegrass is to germinate a sample on filter paper. If there is any fluorescence when exposed to ultraviolet light, the presence of annual ryegrass (or a hybrid of annual and perennial ryegrass) is established. To date, only the Manhattan Ryegrass Growers Association requires this test of quality to be indicated on the seed tab, by calling the fluorescing seedlings "Other crop."

Germination to establishment: how long?

It will be repeated several times in this book that post-seeding care, especially watering, is the single most important factor in deciding the success or failure of a seeded lawn. The trick is to water enough to keep the soil moist, but not so much the soil washes away. This delicate nurturing period, when watering can be a several-times-a-day chore, extends between the time the seed is sown and the point when the grass becomes established. You might wonder how long this period will last? The answer to this question depends on the type of grass, its rate of germination, and initial growth, and the daily temperature. To illustrate this, we conducted an experiment at the Ortho Test Garden in St. Helena, California.

Four grasses were sown the same day: 'Manhattan' perennial ryegrass, 'Merion' Kentucky bluegrass, 'Fortress' creeping red fescue, and common bermudagrass. The photographs at the right, taken at 15 day intervals, show what happened.

Actually, the rate of germination surprised us. The 'Manhattan' ryegrass came up in less than five days. The others were also faster than expected. This extra fast germination was probably due to an unexpected heat wave during the first week that sent temperatures into the mid-nineties. Seed invariably germinates more slowly in the cool temperatures of late fall or early spring.

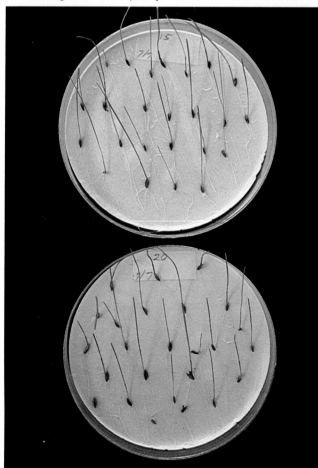
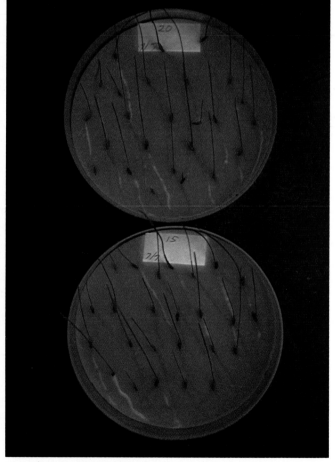

Germinating a sample of improved ryegrass on filter paper (left) is a simple test of purity. If any of the germinating seeds show fluorescence when exposed to ultraviolet light, it confirms the presence of annual ryegrass (right).

Germination time sequence: Four different grasses are sown in identical soil mixes and lightly covered with a mulch. From left to right: 'Manhattan,' 'Merion,' 'Fortress,' and common bermudagrass.

'Manhattan' ryegrass was the first to germinate, followed closely by 'Fortress' fescue. Both the common bermudagrass and 'Merion' Kentucky bluegrass took between 13 and 14 days to emerge.

'Manhattan' and 'Fortress' showed faster growth rates compared to the bermuda and the bluegrass. The most rapid growth after germination of any type grass occurs if the soil is rich in nutrients and the time of year is most favorable.

The new lawn

A beautiful new lawn can have a dramatic effect on a home or building. Landscape plantings are accentuated, and the strong lines of walls, driveways, and sidewalks are softened by an expanse of grass.

With the goal of a lush, green lawn in mind, it is easy to hurry through the initial steps of establishment, but nothing could be more unfortunate. Your first decisions and procedures will be most important to the future of your lawn.

Answers to questions like "Which grass should I plant? . . Do I want to sow seed or use sod, sprigs, stolons or plugs? . . How will I water? . .", all should be fully thought out in advance of any labor. It's a good idea to look through this entire book before beginning work. A little forethought will save you a lot of future headaches.

Ten steps toward a new lawn

We've seen many different ways of getting from bare ground to a new lawn. Some people simply spread seed over their existing ground without preparing the soil. Few lawns started this way succeed, or at the least reach their optimum appearance level. New techniques such as hydromulching are becoming increasingly popular. (See photo.) Regardless of the planting method, success is still measured by long term results.

Here we list the steps of site preparation that lead to a long lasting, beautiful lawn. Following a logical order of events prevents costly backtracking and repetition of similar steps.

1. Test soil
2. Remove debris
3. Control persistent weeds
4. Rough grade the site

5. Add high phosphorus starter fertilizer and lime or sulfur (if necessary)
6. Add soil amendments or top soil, if needed
7. Cultivate thoroughly
8. Install underground irrigation
9. Final grade the site and settle excavation areas
10. Lightly roll

Soil sense

Much of the success of your lawn will depend on how you prepare the soil. It helps to remember that, unlike a vegetable garden where the soil can be rebuilt each year, grass roots utilize the same soil year after year. Although most nutrient deficiencies can be corrected after the lawn has been established, changing the soil struc-

ture under growing grass is difficult and expensive. The time and effort you put into preparing the growing medium will be reflected in the health and beauty of your lawn for years to come. This is true for lawns grown from seed as well as vegetative plantings such as sod. Even though sod has a little soil already attached, site preparation is still critical to success.

Gardeners describe soil types in many ways — heavy, light, clay, sandy, loamy, rich loam, poor soil, lean soil. Scientists and horticulturists classify soils by the proportion of sand, silt, and clay they contain. These designations are based on the size of the soil particles, clay being the smallest, silt bigger, and sand the largest. A soil's texture is determined by the blend of these various particles.

Hydromulching is a new and different way to start a new lawn. Seed is mixed with a paper mulch and water, and sprayed through a hose onto the seed bed.

◁

The essence of freshness — new blades of grass, as yet unmowed, glisten with dew in the early morning light.

For proper growth, plants need air in the soil, available moisture (but not standing water), and a supply of mineral nutrients. If soil has plenty of clay, holding on to nutrients is no problem, but the small clay particles that cling closely together hold water, and leave little room for air. Squeezed into a ball, clay soil clings together tightly; water penetration is slow. Drainage is the main problem in clay soils; the lack of which often results in suffocation of plant roots. You know you have a clay soil if it's rock hard when dry and gummy when wet.

Sandy soils have lots of room for air, but moisture and nutrients disappear quickly. Water sinks right into sandy soil without spreading, and dries up in just a few days after watering. When sandy soils are squeezed into a ball, they quickly fall apart when the ball is released.

In between a sandy or clay soil and the one best for plant growth, is a loam soil. It contains a combination of clay, silt, and sand which retains nutrients and water while still allowing sufficient room for air.

Chances are your soil is not the perfect loam, in which case it would benefit from the addition of organic matter. Even if it is an ideal soil, heavy foot traffic or perhaps construction activity around new homes can severely compact it, closing air spaces and restricting water and nutrient penetration. You've seen the effects of compaction in foot paths worn across a lawn.

Improving soil texture

The best way to make either a heavy clay soil or a light sandy soil into a substitute for a rich loam is through the addition of organic matter — not just a little organic matter, but lots of it.

The addition of organic matter — compost, peat moss, manure, sawdust, shredded ground bark — makes clay soils more friable and easier to work. Organic matter opens up tight clay soils, improves drainage, and allows air to move more readily into the soil. In light sandy soils, organic matter holds moisture and nutrients in the root zone. The more organic matter you add to a sandy soil, the more you increase its moisture-holding capacity.

Enough organic matter should be added to physically change the structure of the soil to a depth of 6 to 8 inches — the area where most grass roots grow. The final soil mixture should be 30 percent organic matter by volume — about 2 inches of organic matter mixed into the top 6 inches of soil is usually sufficient.

A common problem for many homeowners is determining the total amount of organic matter needed to amend their entire lawn area. The chart on page 29 will assist in that calculation.

The type of organic material used depends a great deal on what is locally available. While decomposed barnyard manure and compost are very good, they often contain troublesome weed seeds. Peat moss is generally problem free and available, but also expensive.

Other types of organic materials commonly found in the South include peanut hulls, cotton screenings, shredded tobacco stems, and ground pine bark.

The first step — testing the soil

The first step in preparing any soil for a future lawn is to have your soil tested. Many state universities test soils for a nominal fee. In other areas it may be necessary to go to a private soil testing laboratory.

In the chapter entitled "Lawns in your area" beginning on page 80, specific information on local soil conditions of the South are listed by states. Of the 12 southern states, all provide soil tests through universities.

A soil test eliminates guessing the amounts of nutrients and lime to be added and often provides useful information on the soil's texture. Some give specific recommendations, others supply instructions on how to interpret results and take appropriate steps. If you have any unanswered questions, consult your County Extension Agent.

How to take a soil test

First of all, obtain any necessary forms and questionnaires from your local Cooperative Extension Service office or private soil lab. Information supplied through these forms will assist the lab in making specific recommendations for your site. Typical questions are: "How large is the sample area? Has fertilizer or lime ever been added? To what degree is the land sloped?"

To collect the soil, you will need a clean non-metal bucket or container, a soil sampler, garden trowel or spade, pencil and paper, and a mailable container that will hold about a pint of soil.

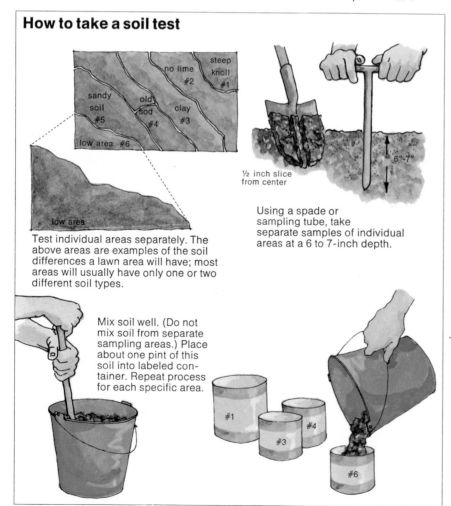

How to take a soil test

no lime #2 steep knoll #1

sandy soil #5 old sod #4 clay #3

low area #6

low area

Test individual areas separately. The above areas are examples of the soil differences a lawn area will have; most areas will usually have only one or two different soil types.

½ inch slice from center

6"-7"

Using a spade or sampling tube, take separate samples of individual areas at a 6 to 7-inch depth.

Mix soil well. (Do not mix soil from separate sampling areas.) Place about one pint of this soil into labeled container. Repeat process for each specific area.

#1 #4 #3 #6

To get reliable soil test results, you must take a representative sample. This means the soil should be gathered from 15 to 20 spots in any one sampling area. Low spots, trouble spots, and areas with obvious soil type differences should be treated as separate sampling areas.

Soil samples should be taken to a depth of 6 to 7 inches, ideally with a soil sampling tube. The hollow shaft of an old golf club or curtain rod will usually suffice. If you don't have a sampler, dig a V-shaped hole 6 to 7 inches deep with a spade or garden trowel. Remove a ½-inch slice from the smooth side. Soil samples from one sampling area should be mixed together thoroughly in the bucket. Allow to dry before proceeding.

Place about a pint of this soil in a sturdy carton or plastic bag, label it properly, and mail it to the soil lab. Record where each sample was taken. Also provide any additional information on the history of the land, if pertinent.

Preparation of the planting site

The amount of work necessary to prepare the soil prior to seeding or sodding obviously depends on its present condition. If you are lucky enough to have a rich loam soil and a proper grade, little may need to be done beyond thorough tilling, fertilizing, and raking. Usually though, more work will be required.

To start with, clear all debris from the planting area. Rotting wood can cause low spots as it decomposes and can serve as a food source for termites. Stones and cement can damage tillers and other equipment.

It is also a good idea to determine the dimensions of your lawn area with a tape measure. Methods for figuring lawn dimensions are explained on page 96. These figures will be useful later in deciding how much amendments to add to the soil.

Next, establish a rough grade by filling low spots and leveling hills. On most lots there are fixed grade points such as house foundations, sidewalks, driveways, and trees. When grading, both rough and finished soil must be distributed so elevation changes between fixed points are gradual.

The ideal grade is a 1 to 2 percent slope away from the house to avoid water drainage toward the foundation. That's about a 1 to 2-foot drop per 100 feet. A long string and a level will be useful in determining the slope.

If the slope is not made to order, rough grading should be done before top soil or amendments are added. This will ensure good uniform soil to the depth of the root zone once the soil has been corrected. If the original soil is acceptable but the grade is wrong, the top 6 inches should be removed, the grade corrected, and the soil returned.

In areas where underlying hardpan or heavy clay soils prevent proper drainage, drain tiles may need to be installed. If this is the case, consult a competent drainage contractor for advice. Drainage work should be done after the rough grade has been established, but before top soil and amendments have been added for the final grade.

If soil is to be moved or placed around trees, take precautions not to disturb roots. Trees in the lawn deserve special care. For further advice, see the section, "Lawn tips," pages 92 to 93.

While working on the rough grade, you should also begin thinking of ways to make later lawn care easier. Header boards and mowing strips accent landscaping lines as well as help contain vigorous grass species.

Once the grade is sloped the way you want it, add the organic material so the final 6 to 8 inches of soil is about 30 percent organic matter. If top soil is replaced or added, spread half of it over the area and thoroughly till it in. This creates a transition zone between underlying soil and new soil. After you have done this, add the other half.

If you plan to install sod, keep in mind the final grade should be about one inch lower than the grade for a seeded lawn, so the sod will fit flush against sprinklers and sidewalks.

Next, add starter fertilizer (high phosphorous) and if the soil test indicates, lime or sulphur. Thoroughly till the soil.

It's important to carefully mix the top 6 to 8 inches of soil. Make several passes with the tiller in opposite directions to ensure soil, organic matter, and fertilizer are properly blended.

Once everything is mixed, it's time to install underground irrigation, if that is what you have decided upon. Waiting until all the tilling is finished will avoid potential damage to pipes.

(continued on page 32)

Mulch coverage in cubic yards

Sq. Ft. of Area	Thickness of mulch						
	⅛"	¼"	½"	1"	2"	3"	4"
1,000'	.39	.78	1.56	3.12	6.24	9.36	12.48
2,000'	.78	1.56	3.12	6.24	12.48	18.72	24.96
3,000'	1.17	2.34	4.68	9.36	18.72	28.08	37.44
4,000'	1.56	3.12	6.24	12.48	24.96	37.44	49.92
5,000'	1.95	3.90	7.80	15.60	31.20	46.80	62.40
10,000'	3.90	7.80	15.60	31.20	62.40	93.60	124.80
20,000'	7.80	15.60	31.20	62.40	124.80	187.20	249.60
40,000'	15.60	31.20	62.40	124.80	249.60	374.40	499.20

Three cubic feet will cover 36 square feet to a depth of one inch.
There are 27 cubic feet in a cubic yard.

Approximate amounts of ground limestone needed to raise pH

Change in pH desired	Pounds of ground limestone per 1,000 square feet*				
	Sand	Sandy loam	Loam	Silt loam	Clay loam
4.0 to 6.5	60	115	161	193	230
4.5 to 6.5	51	96	133	161	193
5.0 to 6.5	41	78	106	129	152
5.5 to 6.5	28	60	78	92	106
6.0 to 6.5	14	32	41	51	55

*In the southern and coastal states, reduce the application by approximately one-half.

Approximate amounts of soil sulfur to lower pH

Change in pH desired	Pounds of sulfur per 1,000 square feet		
	Sand	Loam	Clay
8.5 to 6.5	46	57	69
8.0 to 6.5	28	34	46
7.5 to 6.5	11	18	23
7.0 to 6.5	2	4	7

Carefully rake and level the seedbed 1

Use a steel rake for final grading and removal of stones. In large areas, a piece of chain link fence or wooden drag can be especially helpful in leveling. Take your time on this step — it will prevent scalping from lawn mowers and water puddles from occurring later on. Correcting the grade after the lawn is established is difficult.

Sow the seed 2

Grass seed can be sown with the same equipment used to spread fertilizer if the spreaders are calibrated to distribute seed at recommended rates. As long as you don't drastically over or under seed, the results will be the same. Lawn seed can also be sown by hand.

Regardless of the seeding method, divide the seed into two equal lots. The second lot should be seeded at right angles to the first, covering the entire lawn area in each pass. When using wheeled spreaders it may be necessary to touch up edges by hand.

Lightly rake the seed in and roll 3

To ensure good contact between seed and soil lightly rake the entire area with a rake. Be sure not to rake the area too roughly, this can redistribute seed or ruin the final grade. Hard raking can also bury grass seed too deep. A depth of ⅛ inch to ¼ inch (depending on seed size) is usually considered good for seeding.

4 Add mulch

Mulching the area where grass seed has been sown will hasten germination by keeping soil moist, while also providing protection for young seedlings. On slopes, mulching can be useful in preventing soil erosion while watering.

Many materials can be used as mulches. Here, a thin layer of peat moss is applied with a peat applicator available at local rental yards. In areas that have abundant rainfall or strong winds, a heavier mulch is advisable. Although wind is often a problem with light-weight mulches, various types of netting are available to solve this problem.

The mulch covering should be thin enough to expose some of the soil of the seedbed. Never completely cover the area. If light mulches such as peat are used, follow it up with a rolling. Rollers are usually available on loan from nurseries, or at rental yards. Rollers should be one-fourth to one-half full of water to provide the necessary weight.

5 Water thoroughly

Improper watering probably causes more failures in a newly seeded lawn than any other one factor. For even germination, the very top layer of soil (always the first to dry out) must stay constantly moist. A thorough soaking is required after sowing and then as many as three to four light sprinklings by hand each day until the young grass is established. How long establishment takes depends on the variety of species of grass, the time it takes to germinate, its rate of growth, and daily weather. More frequent watering will be required if it is hot or windy.

Water with a fine spray or mist-type nozzle to minimize moving soil or washing seed away. Avoid standing water.

Stringing the area with brightly colored flags will warn neighbors and children, but not necessarily dogs, to stay off.

Weed control

You will save yourself time and trouble later on if you take steps to eliminate weeds now. There are several methods; most will take at least a month to be effective, and safe.

Methyl bromide completely sterilizes the soil but is very dangerous and should only be used by professionals.

Metham, known under the trade name Vapam, is a useful pre-plant fumigant that requires 30 days to pass after treatment before you can seed.

30 days delay before seeding

If time is not a factor, you can keep the prepared seedbed wet, allowing weed seeds to germinate, and then kill them with a contact herbicide. Or, allow the soil to dry and lightly rake the surface to kill new seedlings as they emerge. Let the soil dry completely before watering again. If this is done three or four times, most of the weeds will be killed, leaving fewer weeds to compete with the grass seedlings.

Be sure to read the labels of all these chemicals carefully. Do not sow any seed until the chemicals have dissipated. Check to see if the soil is safe by planting some quick germinating seeds such as radishes. If they come up and begin normal growth, it's safe to sow seed or lay sod.

Be very careful around trees and shrubs. Many of these chemicals will kill them as well. Read the label!

Final grading

Final grading should be done just prior to planting. The smooth bed can be ruined if it is left too long.

Take time raking and smoothing the area to be sure it is free of rocks and as level as possible. Correcting high and low spots later will be difficult. In large areas a chain or wooden drag can be helpful.

Starting from seed

Regardless of the quick effect of sodding, certain pleasures are afforded to the person who chooses to start a new lawn from sprigs, stolons, or seed. Few colors are as bright yet as soft as young green grass. Growth occurs so quickly that the feeling of actually growing something is more intense; the part you play seems more important. The person who grows his own lawn feels "more the gardener."

To be sure that planting your lawn from seed is a pleasant experience, you should become familiar with lawn seed, how it is packaged, mixed, and the rates at which it is sown. Read about lawn seed on pages 20 to 25.

The time of year you seed is important. Cool-season grasses such as the bluegrasses and fescues, common in northern parts of the South, are best planted in late summer or early fall. Allow four to six weeks before the first frost so the grass can be established before the onset of cold weather.

Starting with vegetative forms

The warm-season grasses, which are most often used in the South, are usually planted by vegetative means such as sprigs, stolons, or sod. This is the case with St. Augustine, zoysia, and hybrid bermudagrass. Common bermuda and centipedegrass, however, are often planted by seed. Sow seed of warm-season grasses in late spring or early summer.

Cool-season grasses can be sown in spring and warm-season grasses in late summer, but planting at these times of the year send young grass right into weather less than ideal for active growth. Cool-season grasses may go dormant in warm weather, warm-season grasses go dormant when it turns cool. Weeds may not follow this schedule and can take over before your new lawn is established. Never sow in the heat of summer — watering at that time will become almost a full time job.

With proper grass selection and care, attaining a beautiful lawn is not as difficult and time consuming as it may seem.

Watering

There are probably more questions asked about watering than any other aspect of lawn care, and rightly so. As it is for any plant, water is one of grass's most basic requirements. Without it, of course, your lawn would not survive.

Watering your lawn would be simple if there were set rules for every situation on exactly how much water to apply and how often, but there are too many variables. Your lawn's water requirements depend on several things: the type of soil you have, the climate of your area, temperatures, wind velocity, humidity, the frequency of rain, the type of turf being used, and maintenance practices.

Even with all these particulars, rules do seem to surface upon reading many lawn books and university extension bulletins. After you have watered your lawn for a while, your own experiences and conditions will lead to some of these apparent rules.

It's important to understand that a good lawn watering program is dependent upon you, the waterer. By getting to know your lawn through close observation and by understanding your local climate characteristics, you can begin to answer many of the important questions yourself.

How often should a lawn be watered?

The answer to this question is simply, when it needs it. A lawn has to be watered when the soil begins to dry out, before the grass actually wilts. At that stage, areas of the lawn will begin to change color, picking up a blue-green or smoky tinge. An even more evident signal is a loss of resilience — footprints will make a long-lasting imprint instead of bouncing right back.

Soil moisture testers and coring tubes are other ways to check for adequate moisture. There are two types of moisture testers — mechanical and electrical. The mechanical type, called a tensionmeter, has a porous tip and a water-filled tube. Water in the tube can be pulled out by dry soil. The suction created is measured on the gauge. Tensionmeters are left in place, once installed. The electrical type operates on the principle that wet soil conducts electricity better than dry soil. A coring tube takes a plug of your lawn and the underlying soil. It allows you to see and feel the moisture level of your lawn's soil.

How long your lawn can go between waterings depends on several things. Roots grow only where there is water. If you constantly wet the top few inches of soil, roots won't venture any deeper. Eventually, the limited size of the root system will force you into watering more often. That means trouble, because frequent watering keeps the surface wet, ideal for weeds and diseases. If roots go deep into the soil, they can draw on a larger water supply and the lawn can go much longer between waterings.

Soil conditions can also affect how often you need to water. For example, 12 inches of loam soil will hold about an inch and a half of water, a sandy soil about half that much, and a clay soil twice as much. Lawns in sandy soil will need water more often than those in a rich loam. Lawns in a clay soil will need water less often, and it will have to be applied at slower rates to avoid wasteful runoff.

Different types of grasses have different water requirements which also affect watering frequency. Grasses are listed according to their drought tolerance on page 19.

Local weather patterns are also important. Seasonal rain can play an integral part in a watering program. When it's hot and windy, it's obvious more frequent watering is required.

Watering during drought

In parts of the South blessed with ample rain, irrigation may only need to be supplementary. In fact, around New Orleans for instance, some areas receive so much water that drainage is the big problem.

In northern parts of the South, cool-season grasses like Kentucky bluegrass or fescue, usually go dormant in the hottest months of summer, returning to full vigor in cooler fall weather. If you want to keep your cool-season grass green in summer and you have started a watering program in the spring, continue it throughout the summer. If the lawn does go dormant, let it stay that way. Too many fluctuations between dormancy and active growth can weaken a lawn.

In drier parts of the South like sections of west Texas, periods of drought are common. Here are some tips on using water efficiently during drought periods.

1. Do not apply fertilizer to lawns when drought conditions exist.

2. Mow your grass higher and less often. However, don't let it grow a third more than its recommended mowing height.

3. Reduce weed competition.

4. Irrigate without runoff to root zone depth (about 6 to 8 inches), and only when your lawn shows the need.

Here, sprays of sparkling water refresh more than the lawn.

In order to water efficiently, you need to know your sprinkler's pattern and rate of distribution. Evenly spaced containers on the lawn area show how much water falls in specific areas. In our test, the stationary fan type applied water unevenly.

These tips are not normal lawn care practices. Under a system of survival irrigation, a lawn may develop a spotty, thinned apearance. Another alternative, although drastic, is to let the lawn die out altogether and replant with a more drought-resistant turf when suitable weather returns.

On pages 80 to 87 are local weather characteristics for southern climates. They should be helpful in setting up your specific watering program. Rain gauges are also useful. By knowing how much rain has fallen, you can tell how much supplemental water is needed. Don't be misled by light drizzles that supply very little soil moisture. Watering right after a light shower, however, may be an effective way of reducing water use.

How much water does a lawn need?

To keep grass roots growing deeply, the soil should be moistened to a depth of about 6 to 8 inches. This should take between 1 and 2 inches of water over the lawn surface. Depending on the weather and the soil type, the average lawn will deplete this amount of water in about one week. To tell if the water has gone down that deep, wait 12 hours and check with a soil sampler. Or, simply poke a screw-driver into the ground. If it penetrates about 6 inches without much resistance, the lawn is usually wet enough.

Water should be applied as uniformly as possible, and no faster than the soil can absorb it. Avoid applying so much at one time that it results in wasteful runoff. If this occurs, divide your watering into timed intervals. Sprinkle until the soil can't take anymore and stop for 20 or 30 minutes to allow for absorption. Continue until the desired amount has been applied.

What time of day should the lawn be watered?

This question has been answered in many ways, not all of them correct. Some suggest that afternoon watering causes sun scald of the grass blades. This has proven to be false. Others suggest that moisture left on a lawn overnight from a late afternoon or evening watering promotes disease. In both cases, these statements, need to be qualified.

First of all, there are several disadvantages to afternoon watering. At that time, evaporation caused by the wind and sun are at a maximum. Also, less of the water applied is actually made available to the lawn. Wind can disrupt sprinkler patterns, causing poor coverage. Local water consumption is usually highest in the afternoon which can result in low water pressure. Keep in mind, too, that drought symptoms are more evident in the afternoons and evenings. These symptoms can be induced by the higher temperatures and winds typical of that time of day, but are not always an indication of water stress. Often the grass will regain its color as temperatures and winds subside.

Whether or not afternoon or evening watering promotes disease is still under some debate among experts, but it shouldn't cause any uncertainty in your watering program. Most lawns become wet at night naturally by dew. Cultural practices such as proper fertilizing, regular dethatching, and mowing at recommended heights will do more to prevent disease than watering at times other than in the afternoon. If you feel a wet lawn at night is increasing disease problems, water in the early morning rather than evening. This will save water and your lawn will have less moisture at night.

Early morning, then, is an ideal time to water, but the answer to the question "when" still remains: *water when the lawn needs it.*

Watering new lawns

There is a different set of rules for watering a newly seeded or sodded lawn. Sprinkling is, at the least, an everyday requirement. The germination of seed or the knitting of sod roots to new soil will often require watering more than once a day. We've discussed new lawn watering in detail on page 29.

Portable sprinklers

As we said previously, you have to understand your lawn's requirements and signals. It is equally true you must be very familiar with your sprinkling equipment. Whether you choose a reliable, portable sprinkler, or an automatic, underground system, the rates at which the water is applied and the pattern of water distribution will vary. Automatic systems, if properly designed and installed, are usually more precise and predictable. If you do choose to water with portable sprinklers, look over the many types with a skeptical eye, and a thought for uniform coverage and minimum water waste.

There are many types of portable sprinklers, so consequently, there are many patterns of water distribution. Even individual sprinklers of the same type can have completely different patterns. Without knowing this, a very conscientious waterer can end up with over and under-watered sections of lawn. This produces uneven green and brown areas, and unnecessary weeds and disease. Along with knowledge of soil and climate conditions, sprinkler patterns and water distribution are very important aspects of watering.

The container test

There is an easy way to measure sprinkler water distribution. Set up a gridlike pattern of small (same size) containers on a section of the lawn. The grid pattern may change for different types of sprinklers, but it's a good idea to start with a straight line of containers, extending them at set intervals, from close to the sprinkler head, to just outside the reach of the water. Turn the sprinkler on at the pressure you would normally operate for a set time and then record the amount of water deposited in each container. This will give you a good idea of the sprinkler pattern, as well as the amount of water distributed.

Realizing that a lawn needs about an inch or so of water per week, you can easily tell how long a sprinkler should be run and to what degree the pattern should be overlapped for efficient watering.

We bought 15 of the major types of sprinklers and measured their pat-

Overlapping sprinkler patterns helps apply an even distribution.
With overlapping, this whirling head sprinkler becomes efficient.
Occasional hand watering assures even coverage.

terns of water distribution using the testing method described previously. It is important to repeat there can be variations between sprinklers of the same type, especially those made by different manufacturers. It is best to check your own sprinkler to be certain of its distribution and pattern.

The most inefficient sprinkler tested was the stationary fan type. Rates of water accumulating in the containers varied from 8 inches an hour in one spot, to 2 inches an hour just 4 feet away, to almost nothing very close to the sprinkler head. There was seemingly no predictable pattern that could lead to proper overlapping and efficient watering. However, to label the

fan-type sprinkler useless is unfair. As long as the water distribution is known, they can be valuable for spot watering or as a supplement to other types of sprinklers.

We also tested the popular oscillating-arm sprinkler. Many believe this sprinkler deposits maximum amounts of water near the sprinkler, the decreasing quantities towards the periphery as the arm moves farthest from vertical. We found this to be true of older models, but discovered a different story when we tested a newer model from a different manufacturer. The newer sprinkler stalls momentarily when the arm is farthest from vertical, thus depositing more water near

Oscillating-arm sprinklers are designed to apply water
over large areas, and are highly adjustable. Individual sprinklers differ;
test yours to be certain of its pattern.

the periphery of the pattern to even out the distribution. This demonstrates the need to test each individual sprinkler.

A third model tested was the whirling-head type. It deposited the largest amount of water close to the sprinkler and decreasing amounts at greater distances from the source of the spray. When this type of sprinkler is used without overlapping, water distribution is uneven. With a 50 percent overlap, its efficiency is increased and the sprinkler becomes quite useful.

Combining a little knowledge gained from experimentation and an observant eye, setting up a watering schedule with a portable sprinkler can be quite easy.

Get to know your lawn

As you become more adept at observation, you will become the watering expert for your lawn. By paying attention to your lawn's signals, a regular watering schedule will unfold, but with you in charge, compensating for changes in weather and the passing of the seasons.

Certain areas of the lawn will consistently signal water need before others. It may be an area on a slight slope facing south with maximum sun that always dries out first. Or it may be an area exposed to more wind than others. These spots are clues, and will mark the time to begin watering. Hand watering isolated dry areas can sometimes extend waterings a day or two.

Developing a water efficient lawn

There are other cultural practices besides watering deeply and less frequently that will increase your watering efficiency. Two major problems that result in poor water penetration are thatch and compacted soil. If bad enough, either one can actually repel water, causing wasteful runoff. Regular dethatching and aerification as described on pages 57 to 59, increase water penetration, provide air in the root zone, and aid in nutrient uptake.

Following recommended mowing heights or mowing even higher in hot summer months will also conserve water.

Proper fertilization is another important factor in efficient watering. Poor fertilization invites competition from water-hungry weeds, and reduces the wear-and-tear capacity of the lawn. On the other hand, over-fertilization promotes vigorous water-hungry growth of the lawn which can cause thatch to develop.

About that hose

Most gardeners realize that a hose can be their best friend or their worst enemy. Improper use, or a hose of poor quality can do more harm than good. Does your hose have leaky connections? Is it impossible to roll it up? Is it long enough?

If you answered yes to any one of these questions, you probably need to make minor repairs or purchase a new hose. Repair is easy and inexpensive. On the other hand, although a high quality hose is more expensive, it will provide excellent service for a long time.

A well-made hose will be flexible in any weather. This is usually the case with high grade rubber and laminated filament hoses. It is seldom true of inexpensive plastic models. The hose you buy should be long enough to reach all areas of your yard, and have a large enough diameter to supply sufficient quantities of water. The larger the diameter of the hose, the more water it can deliver. Home garden variety hoses are available in ¾ inch, ⅝ inch and ½ inch diameters. The ⅝ inch is a usual choice for a medium-sized lawn area.

If your hose needs repair, there is a wide variety of hose repair equipment available, from clamp-on to screw-on kits. Our favorite is the brass screw-on type shown below.

If you have ever damaged plants when dragging the hose around, consider heavy wooden stakes in key areas of the garden.

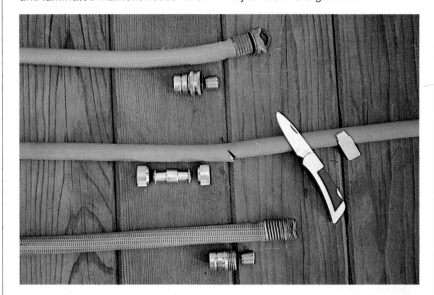

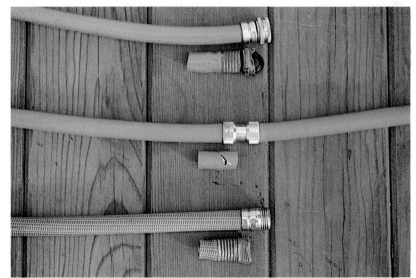

Too many gardeners put up with broken or leaky hoses without realizing how easy and inexpensive they are to repair. The photo above shows some of the more common hose problems. Below, are the same hoses after being repaired.

Underground irrigation

The interest in underground irrigation systems seems to increase every year. The advantages over portable sprinklers are many, but the most obvious is the convenience of not having to constantly move sprinklers. In the majority of cases, they are also more efficient. Sprinkler heads apply predictable amounts of water over an exact area, eliminating the most objectional grievance of portable sprinklers — uneven water distribution. An underground system combined with an automatic timer can even water while you're away from home. It's important to stress that a poorly designed or poorly installed underground system will be just as bad or worse than a portable sprinkler.

The one disadvantage of an underground system is the initial cost of materials and the installation labor. But along with the increased interest in such systems, materials have become cheaper as well as easier to install. Galvanized steel and copper pipe have gradually given way to lightweight PVC (Poly Vinyl Chloride) plastic pipe and flexible polyethylene pipe. Heavy wrenches required to fit metal pieces together have been replaced by easy-to-use glue. Manufacturers have spent time and money in the production of simplified directions for home owners who wish to do the work themselves.

Information for home installation

It is impossible in a book this size to give full, detailed information on how to install an underground irrigation system. Materials differ greatly between manufacturers, and there are too many variables for each specific site. What we have done is outline a typical underground installation. We've indicated where the problems might arise, how they can be solved, and the different types of equipment that can fit ideally into specific situations.

Choose the manufacturer as well as the supplier carefully. Consult neighbors who have underground systems, talk to irrigation specialists, nurserymen, or your County Extension Agent to get help in selecting a trade name that will best suit your needs. You can then either write the manufacturer, or obtain the available installation aids and catalogs from a local distributor.

Installing a sprinkler system, step by step

STEP 1
Install valve system
☐ Assemble valve assembly with PVC adapters in advance.
☐ Cut in tee for sprinkler main.
☐ Dig trench to valves.
☐ Install and flush valves.
☐ Check for leaks.

Step 2
Stake layout of system
☐ Use stakes and string to mark sprinkler heads and pipe trench locations.

Step 3
Dig trenches
☐ Use a flat-edged spade to dig v-shaped trenches (5" wide at the top and 6-8" deep).

Step 4
Assemble PVC pipe
☐ Solvent-weld PVC pipe and fittings.
☐ Wait 12 hours.
☐ Insert plastic risers.
☐ Flush out pipe lines.
☐ Install sprinkler heads.

STEP 5
Test for coverage
☐ Turn on each valve and be sure entire area is covered properly.
☐ Lower pop-up heads to proper level.

STEP 6
Backfill trenches
☐ Fill trenches a little higher than the final soil line.
☐ Soak the soil to allow for settling.
☐ Check final leveling.

One thing to realize at the very start and its importance cannot be overemphasized, is the manufacturer of the system being installed will be your most helpful friend. Most will provide completely illustrated, easy-to-follow instructions that are useful not only to the individual who wants to do the entire job himself, but also to anyone who wishes to contract the job out to an irrigation specialist.

Begin with a plan

After you've decided to put in an underground irrigation system, you need to decide how much (if any) of the work you are going to do yourself. Companies specializing in irrigation can often install a system within hours, and in no more than a few days. Do-it-yourself installation may take several weekends. If the sprinklers are to be installed prior to planting a new lawn, the clutter of equipment may mean nothing. In an established lawn it may be bothersome, or even damaging. Cost is also a consideration. If you are handy with tools and have the time, it is much cheaper to do it yourself.

However you decide, remember the importance of choosing reliable specialists to assist you.

Begin your sprinkler system with graph paper (10 grids to an inch is fine), a soft lead pencil, a dime store compass, and a measuring tape. A plan on paper will help you install a better system. Besides, a carefully prepared plan helps when ordering materials, makes it easier to get advice from your garden center, irriga-

tion specialist, or hardware dealer, and serves as a record as to where the pipelines are laid.

Make your plan complete. A good plan is actually a bird's-eye view of your property drawn to scale, preferably 1 inch equaling 20 feet. With that scale, you should be able to fit all important details on a 8½ by 11-inch piece of paper. It should show all construction and landscape features which could affect the design and installation of the sprinkler system. This includes shrubs and trees, paved areas, fencing, and less apparent objects such as mailboxes, raised planters, and buried drainage or power lines. If significant, it is also helpful to note prevailing wind direction, sun and shade areas, steep slopes, as well as high and low spots in your landscape.

Draw the plan for both the front and back yards, even if you plan to install the system in only one area. You may want a similar system in another area at a later date. If you want to include sprinklers for trees and shrubs, indicate any water-sensitive or especially thirsty plants on the plan.

An important number — gallons per minute

One of the most important aspects of building a successful sprinkler system is determining the available water in gallons per minute. This is usually abbreviated GPM. The best way to find available GPM is to use a gauge. A GPM gauge automatically compensates for friction loss, pipe corrosion, and similar variables. Most sprinkler suppliers will loan this gauge upon request.

It is possible to deduce available GPM without the use of this gauge. First, check the water meter size. It should be stamped on the meter itself. If it isn't, ask your local water company. Common meter sizes are ⅝ inch, ¾ inch, and 1 inch. Next, determine your static water pressure with a gauge measured in pounds per square inch (PSI). These gauges are much more commonly available than the GPM gauge. When figuring static pressure, use an outside faucet connected to the service line, and have all inside water turned off. Last, find out the size of the service line from your meter to the house.

Types of pipe

Ease of handling, assembly, durability, flow characteristics, cost, and availability are reasons to recommend PVC pipe and solvent-welded fittings as the piping for sprinkler installations. Schedule 40 PVC is normally sold in 20-foot lengths. Use the heavy-duty schedule 40 for all pressure-holding lines. To save money and materials, use class 200 or class 315 pipe for all lateral lines that will never be required to hold constant pressure.

Flexible polyethylene pipe is also acceptable and very easy to use in sprinkler lines, but it cannot handle enough pressure to be used between the water meter and control valves.

The advantage of the flexible pipe is that you're not restricted to straight lines. Polypipe comes in 100-foot or 200-foot rolls and can be cut with a knife. Fittings are inserted into the pipe and held in place with stainless steel clamps tightened with a screwdriver or wrench.

Sprinkler heads

While a wide variety of sprinkler heads are available for every conceivable application, most residential lawns and gardens can be best served by using adjustable, pop-up lawn sprinkler heads with full, half circle, and quarter circle watering patterns. When not in use, the head rests flush to the ground, out of the way of mower and foot traffic. It is important to remember that each sprinkler head is designed to discharge a specific number of gallons per minute (GPM) over a given radius, and that each head requires a certain water pressure in order to achieve its designed throw.

When adjusting the arc of a sprinkler head, check specifications to see that this does not drastically affect the rate at which the water is applied to the lawn (precipitation rate). This could change your watering strategy.

Square pattern and low precipitation rate heads are also available. Square patterns are useful in narrow areas such as side yards and parking strips. Use low precipitation heads in areas where runoff is a problem due

to a sloping grade or clay soil.

Besides pop-up spray heads, there are also impulse sprinklers which can be useful in large areas. However, these can be rather difficult to use efficiently in smaller lawns. In center areas of a lawn, especially if wind is a problem, consider pop-up sprinklers with rotary action, dispersing water in large drops rather than a spray.

Drawing sprinklers on your plan

Set your compass to match the radius of the sprinkler heads according to the scale of your plan. Lightly draw in quarter circles wherever a 90° angle is shown within the area to be sprinkled. Next, draw the half-head circles normally located adjacent to paved areas, buildings, and property lines.

Finally, fill in center areas with full circle symbols. There are a variety of arcs available. Many installers have found one or more of these areas to be much more convenient for fitting a sprinkler spray to irregular shaped areas. Overspray can be a problem.

Here are a few good rules to follow.

1. Overlap the outer third of a sprinkler head's spray radius, more if wind is a problem.

2. Cut back the radius of your circles to accommodate design, but do not attempt to stretch it.

3. Design your system so that water is applied from the outside perimeter

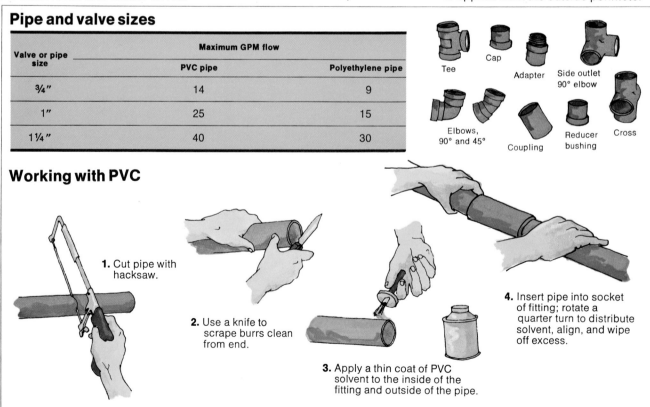

Pipe and valve sizes

Valve or pipe size	Maximum GPM flow	
	PVC pipe	Polyethylene pipe
¾"	14	9
1"	25	15
1¼"	40	30

Tee — Cap — Adapter — Side outlet 90° elbow

Elbows, 90° and 45° — Coupling — Reducer bushing — Cross

Working with PVC

1. Cut pipe with hacksaw.

2. Use a knife to scrape burrs clean from end.

3. Apply a thin coat of PVC solvent to the inside of the fitting and outside of the pipe.

4. Insert pipe into socket of fitting; rotate a quarter turn to distribute solvent, align, and wipe off excess.

inward toward the center.

4. Experiment with various full and part-circle head combinations and spacing patterns, until coverage is complete with no potential dry spots.

5. Water lawns and planted areas separately unless sprinkler heads are designed to deliver optimum amounts of water to the plants.

Control valves

Your irrigation system will have to be divided into circuits which operate one at a time. There will probably not be enough available water pressure to water the entire lawn at once. Each circuit will have a separate control valve. Together all the control valves compose what's called the manifold, which should be placed in a convenient location, usually next to a doorway and out of reach of the sprinkler spray. One manifold each will be needed for both the front and back yard. Draw the manifold in your plan. Try to conceal the manifold with some sort of cover or box as the plumbing is seldom attractive. An anti-siphon valve will prevent backflow of water into the house supply. They are sometimes required by local ordinances and are always a good idea.

Use the three figures obtained earlier (water meter size, static water pressure, size of service line) to determine the gallons per minute available to any one circuit. Group the sprinklers into circuits, making sure the total GPM discharged does not exceed what you've just determined is available. It's all right to have less, but try to keep each circuit about the same. Do not mix different types of sprinkler heads (impulse, spray, shrub bubblers) in one circuit. Take your time planning your different circuits. It may take two or three tries to get it right.

Whenever possible, group sprinkler heads by the requirements of an area. In other words, water sloping areas

Loss due to friction PVC pipe

(pressure drop p.s.i.
per 100 ft. of pipe)

Flow GPM	Pipe size			
	½″	¾″	1″	1¼″
1	.21	.06	.02	
2	.76	.22	.06	
3	1.16	.46	.14	.04
4	2.74	.79	.23	.08
5	4.14	1.19	.35	.10
10		4.29	1.27	.37
15			2.68	.78
20				1.33

with low precipitation heads and windy areas with heads that apply larger drops of water.

Valve and pipe size

Draw the piping in from the valves to the sprinklers. Avoid going under sidewalks and driveways if possible. Split the flow whenever you can so smaller-sized (cheaper) pipe can be used. Pipe size is determined from the maximum number of GPM that can flow through. Use the chart on page 38 to determine pipe and valve size. For example, if a circuit requires 16 GPM, available 1-inch PVC should be used. However, if the flow down the line is reduced to 8 GPM, the pipe size can be reduced to ¾ inch.

Pipe size from the control valve to the supply line should be the size of the largest valve in the system. If the distance between supply line and valves is over 100 feet, go one size larger.

Pressure change due to friction or slope

Two factors can influence the water pressure available to operate a sprinkler head. One is friction — caused when water moves through the pipe. The other is a change in elevation between the water source and the sprinkler head.

Pressure loss due to friction is dependent on the length and size of the pipe and the amount of water traveling through. It is accumulative and can be determined in PSI per 100 feet of pipe. Increasing the pipe size will increase flow and decrease friction. (See chart.)

If your irrigation system runs up a slope, add almost half (.433 to be exact) a pound per square inch of pressure that you need for every foot of rise. If it runs down a slope, subtract this amount for every foot of fall.

Check your plan

At this point you should be ready to begin installation of your underground irrigation system. In order to avoid costly problems, it is a good idea to have your plan checked by a specialist before you begin. The retail dealer who supplies your equipment may offer help, in which case you may have it checked free of charge. Otherwise, it will be money well-spent to engage the services of an independent installer.

Installation

Installation specifics will vary between manufacturers. They should be

spelled out in detail in printed material available from dealers, distributors, or the manufacturer. The basic steps are outlined on page 37.

Cold winter climates

In areas where the soil will freeze in winter, it is necessary to install drain valves at the lowest point in each circuit, as well as between the control valves and the first gate valve near the water meter. The latter will most likely be in the basement. Use a level to avoid any water pockets in the system.

The drain valves in each circuit should be aiming down on a slight tilt, covered with a short piece of pipe, surrounded with gravel and covered with visqueen plastic. Never put a drain valve in a fitting before the fitting is attached to the pipe; PVC solvent may clog the valve.

Riser height and backfill

Before connecting the sprinkler heads, use a ruler to determine the proper length of the riser. This will depend on whether it's an old or new lawn, whether a new lawn is seed or sod, its eventual mowing height, and the height reached by the nozzle of a pop-up sprinkler. If the risers are too long, the sprinkler head may be damaged by mowers, and if too short, they may become clogged with soil. Make them longer if sod will be installed, shorter if you are starting a lawn from seed.

Several types of risers are available to make this easier. A cutaway riser has sections of thread in short increments along its entire length. Small ½-inch pieces are easily cut away one or two at a time until the proper height is reached. Flexible risers require proper height adjustment, but if by accident the sprinkler head is kicked or hit by a mower, they flex rather than break. Repairing underground damage to PVC can be troublesome.

Test your system first, then replace the soil in the trenches and water it thoroughly to settle it in. Repeat as necessary until the trenched area is level with the surrounding soil. This will avoid high and low spots.

Automatic timers

For complete automation in lawn watering, you may want to install an electric timer and automatic valves on your system. Most manufacturers also supply timers.

Locate the timer where it can be protected from sun and rain and close to an electrical outlet; a garage is ideal. Its positioning may influence the location of your control valves.

Sprigs, stolons, and plugs

In the southern United States, where warm-season grasses predominate, starting a lawn by sprigs, stolons, or plugs is a common method of planting. Because most of the warm-season grasses spread horizontally by above-ground stolons (referred to as runners from here on), or underground rhizomes, sections of the plants can be evenly spaced over an area. In time, they will cover, forming a beautiful lawn. This planting method is not practiced with most cool-season grasses.

With some grasses, hybrid bermudagrass for example, planting vegetatively with sprigs, stolons, plugs, or sod is the only possible way because they do not produce viable seed.

The first step to any one of these three methods is to properly prepare the soil according to the instructions beginning on page 28.

Sprigs and stolons

A turf specialist at the University of Florida has this to say about sprigs:

A sprig is an individual stem or piece of a stem of a grass. Regardless of what a sprig is technically, rhizome or stolon, if it has at least one node or joint, it has the potential of developing into a grass plant and spreading. Sprigging is simply the planting of individual sprigs at spaced intervals. A suitable sprig should have roots or at least two to four nodes from which roots can develop.''

Bermuda, zoysia, and bentgrass are commonly planted by this method.

Sprigs can be bought by the bushel or obtained by buying sod and pulling it apart into separate sprigs. If bought by the bushel, they probably will be shipped to you from the point of origin in bags or boxes. Shipping usually takes place within 24 hours after shredding.

The soil should be ready to plant when they arrive. Keep the sprigs cool and moist until planting time, which should be as soon as possible. Only five minutes of sunlight can damage sprigs in plastic bags. Even when stored properly, sprigs will decay rapidly.

There are several ways to plant sprigs. One method is to cut 2 to 3-inch deep furrows in the seed bed, placing the sprigs in the furrows up to 12 inches apart (depending on how fast you want coverage). The furrows can be dug with a hoe and spaced from 4 to 12 inches; again, this depends on the rate of coverage you would like. Close spacing results in more rapid coverage, but naturally involves more material and labor.

If you use the furrow method, place the runners up against one side of the furrow so that any tufts of foliage are above ground, and the light-colored runner is below ground. Firm the soil around it and level the area as well as possible. A light rolling will help firm soil around runners and aid in the leveling.

It's best to begin working with slightly moist soil, but this often causes more problems than it's worth. In any case, *don't let the stolons dry out.* Water sections as you plant them, and keep the soil constantly moist until the runners are established.

Another method of planting sprigs is to place the runners on the soil at desired intervals and lightly press them in with a notched stick.

A third and faster method is called stolonizing, broadcast sprigging, or shredding. The sprigs are broadcast over the area like a mulch, either cut into the soil with a sprigging disc or covered with a mulch or soil and rolled. Peat moss, ground bark, or sawdust work well as mulches—about ¼ inch is satisfactory.

Plugs

Plugging is exactly what it sounds like — small circles or squares of sod are plugged into the soil at regular intervals. Square plugs are cut from sod with a shovel or knife, while round plugs are cut with a special steel plugger similar to a bulb planter. The plugs are placed in corresponding size holes spaced 6 to 12 inches apart in the lawn area. The plugs are then tamped (or rolled) and watered. Although plugs do not dry out as fast as sprigs, keeping the surrounding soil moist is still very important. Coverage from plugs will be slower than sprigging, but less plant material is damaged or lost.

St. Augustine and centipedegrass are usually cut into plugs 3 to 4 inches in diameter and planted on one foot centers. Bermuda and zoysiagrass plugs are usually 2 inches in diameter and planted on 6 or 12 inch centers. Spacing determines the time it will take to achieve complete coverage.

When plugging or sprigging, it is usually necessary to top dress with soil or organic matter after the initial

Planting methods for warm-season grasses

Grass	Method
Bahiagrass	Seed
Bermudagrass:	
Common	Sprigs, Plugs, Sod, Seed
All others	Sprigs, Plugs, Sod
Carpetgrass	Sprigs, Plugs, Sod, Seed
Centipedegrass	Sprigs, Plugs, Sod, Seed
St. Augustinegrass	Sprigs, Plugs, Sod
Zoysiagrass *Z. japonica*	Sprigs, Plugs, Sod
All others	Sprigs, Plugs, Sod

A square yard of sod provides: 2,000 to 3,000 bermuda or zoysiagrass sprigs; 500 to 1,000 St. Augustine or centipedegrass sprigs; 324 two-inch plugs; 84 four-inch plugs; approximately one bushel of sprigs. Row planting requires about 2 to 6 bushels per 1,000 square feet. Broadcast planting requires anywhere from 3 to 10 bushels.

establishment to level the lawn. Irrigation and rain can cause the soil to wash out between sprigs or plugs, yielding an uneven and bumpy lawn.

The best time to plant plugs and sprigs and stolons is just prior to warming days of spring. The onset of warm weather will provide optimum growing conditions for warm-season grasses.

Sprigs are individual grass stems or pieces of stems. Planted at regular intervals, they spread to become a lawn.

Sod lawns

Sod is turf that is grown commercially, cut into strips, and lifted intact with a thin layer of soil held together by the rhizomes, the roots, or netting. Installing a sod lawn is much like laying a carpet, with the objective of reestablishing the grass roots in well-prepared soil.

In the southern and southwestern United States and even coastal areas of the North, plugging or sprigging is the common way to install a lawn. Bermudagrass is available as sprigs, sod, or seed; St. Augustinegrass from stolons, 2-inch sod plugs, or sod; zoysiagrass from sprigs or 2-inch sod plugs, centipedegrass is available as seed, sprigs, or 2-inch sod plugs.

Compared with establishing a lawn by seed, sprigging, or plugging, laying sod yields much quicker results. A sod lawn can be functional in as little as two weeks, although some restraint should be used until its roots are properly knitted with the soil. This can be checked by lifting corners. Under proper conditions, sprigging of bermudagrass may cover in 8 to 10 weeks. Plugging of St. Augustinegrass can take 3 months to cover, and a seed lawn requires 14 to 21 days for germination, followed by a 6- to 10-week establishment period prior to use.

While timing of a seeded lawn is critical, a sod lawn, weather permitting, can be installed almost any time of year. Ideal times to put in sod are late summer and early fall for cool-season grasses, late spring and early summer for warm-season grasses. Cool-season lawns can also be installed in early spring.

Sod can also be installed in areas where a seed lawn may be difficult to establish due to traffic, or on a slope where erosion can be a problem.

The one drawback of sod is the initial cost and the labor involved, which can be substantial compared to a seed lawn. But what price tag can you place on instant results?

Select a high quality sod
The first step is to select a high quality, healthy turf of a grass well adapted to your area and site.

Sod of cool-season grasses is generally available in the same varieties or blends of varieties that can be obtained in seed mixes. Mixtures usually include both shade-tolerant and sun-loving grass types.

Sod usually comes in rolled or folded strips from 6 to 9 feet long and two feet wide. It should be moist but not too wet, and definitely not too dry. If the sod delivered is high quality, it will be uniformly green. Don't buy any sod with poor color or yellowing.

The thickness of different varieties of sod may vary, but generally it should be about ¾ to 1 inch thick. If the sod is too thick, it will root slowly or poorly, too thin, and it will dry out too fast. It should not fall apart easily when handled.

Some states have a sod certification program to insure the sod is labeled correctly, and is relatively free of insects, weeds, and disease. If certified sod is not available, make sure the sod you buy originates from a reputable sod farm.

Important — prepare the soil
Before the sod is delivered the soil should be thoroughly prepared according to the instructions on pages 27 and 28. Don't be fooled into thinking that because sod already has soil attached, that soil preparation is not important. It is just as important as it is with the establishment of a seeded lawn.

After delivery
Sod is usually delivered on pallets to the site where it is to be installed. Once the sod arrives, it should be laid as soon as possible. Do not leave it rolled and stacked on pallets more than one day in hot weather. If it's cool, sod can remain rolled for 2 to 3 days. Store in a cool, shaded area. Be sure to keep the soil on outer pieces moist.

Watering the new sod
Proper watering is the single most important step in the establishment of a sod lawn. Moisten the soil before laying sod. It's best to water a day or two in advance to avoid laying the sod on muddy soil. After the sod is in place, it may be necessary to water every day for up to two weeks until the roots have sufficiently knitted with the underlying soil. If a large area is being sodded it's better to work in sections. Lay the sod in one area, roll and water, then move on to another area. This is much less risky, especially if the weather is warm.

After watering, lift a corner of the sod to be sure the soil underneath is moist. An inch of water over the area is usually sufficient to wet soil and sod. Keep the soil moist at all times but not so wet that it is saturated.

The edges of the sod strips and borders along paths and driveways will be the first to dry out and the last to knit with the soil.

Installing sod on a slope
When laying sod on a slope, start from the lowest point and move uphill. Always lay the sod so it runs perpendicular to the slope and stagger the joints to avoid excess erosion during irrigation or rain.

Pegging or staking sod strips may be desirable on steeper slopes. Three pegs 6 to 8 inches long will usually hold each sod piece in place. Place one peg near each corner and one in the center. Pegs should be driven through the sod vertically, not perpendicular to the slope, near the top edge of the strip.

Mowing and aerification
The time of the first mowing will depend on the species planted. Newly turfed areas should be mowed as soon as the grass is 2½ to 3 inches high. It should be clipped frequently enough to prevent removal of more than one-third of the growth at one mowing. See pages 48 to 51 for further information on mowing.

Aerifying a newly laid sod lawn two or three months after installation will help in the formation of a strong, well rooted turf. Some lawn growers aerify even sooner. Moisture, air, and fertilizer can then pass through the turf more easily, into the root zone where they are needed.

Where sod comes from: A cutting machine lifts strips of turf at a sod farm. Make sure the sod you buy is freshly harvested.

Choose high quality sod 1

Many problems can be avoided if high quality sod of the proper type is purchased. Most states have sod inspection programs to insure that sod is free of weeds, diseases, and insects and that it is the variety or species it is advertised to be. Make sure sod originates from a reputable sod farm. Your County Extension Agent or local nurseryman should be helpful. In addition, many nurseries sell and install sod. See text for other characteristics of healthy sod.

Prepare the soil 2

Because you are laying actively growing grass with good soil already attached, you may think it unnecessary to prepare the soil. Nothing could be more untrue.

Prepare the soil as you would for a seed lawn (see page 28), but make the final grade about an inch lower so sod will fit flush against sidewalks, driveways, and sprinklers. If the soil test indicates, add lime or sulphur.

Take time to make sure the soil is as level as possible, using a drag leveler if necessary. Once the sod is laid it is difficult to level. If large quantities of amendments have been added to parts or all of the future lawn area, wet the soil thoroughly to settle it, allow it to dry, and regrade.

Spread fertilizer and moisten soil 3

If the proper amounts of fertilizer have been worked into the soil during site preparation, it is not usually necessary to fertilize again for 6 weeks or whenever the lawn starts showing the need. If fertilizer has not yet been added, rake in a high phosphorus fertilizer to a depth of 2 or 3 inches.

Sod should be laid on damp soil. Muddy soil causes footprints and uneven spots. Dry soil will lead to drying and eventual weakening of the sod. If the soil is dry, plan to wet it a day or so prior to delivery of the sod so it has adequate time to dry to a damp stage.

4 Keep sod moist

Everything should be ready for installation of the sod prior to its delivery. Sod should not remain rolled or stacked for more than one day in hot weather. In cooler weather it can remain healthy for up to two or three days.

Do not allow the soil on the outer rolls to dry out. Occasionally give the rolls a light sprinkling, but take care not to oversaturate them, or they will be difficult to handle.

5 Start with a straight edge

The easiest way to begin laying sod is to start with a straight edge, such as a sidewalk or driveway. If you have an irregularly shaped lawn, draw a straight line through it or string a line across it, and start laying sod to either side. Handle the sod carefully to avoid tearing.

The rolls of sod are heavy — each strip can weigh as much as 40 pounds. The truck pictured above is loaded to near its weight-carrying capacity. It's best to have two or three helpers ready to help as soon as the truck arrives.

On a hot day (like the day these photographs were taken) it is a good idea to lightly sprinkle the strips as soon as they are laid.

Roll out the sod **6**

Place the loose end of the rolled sod tightly against the previously laid strip and carefully unroll it. Ends of sod pieces should be staggered much like a brick layer staggers the ends of the bricks.

Here's a good tip: when rolling out sod strips, stand or kneel on a board or piece of plywood to distribute your weight. Otherwise, you are likely to end up with pockets and uneven spots.

Place edges tightly together **7**

To avoid unnecessary drying, keep the edges of the sod in as close contact as possible without overlapping. Firm the edges together with your fingers but do not try to stretch the sod.

If the gaps cannot be avoided, fill them with good soil or organic matter and pay close attention to them while watering; they will be the first areas to dry out. Do not attempt to fill small gaps (less than 3 or 4 inches square) with sod because these small pieces of grass usually dry out and die.

Cut pieces to fit with a knife **8**

Along curved edges or unusually shaped areas, custom fit sod using a sharp knife or garden spade to cut the turf. As mentioned in Step 5, it is best to begin with a straight edge and work towards irregular areas.

9 Roll to insure good contact between sod and soil

After all the sod has been laid, roll it with a water-filled roller to ensure good contact between sod roots and underlying soil. It is best to roll perpendicular to the length of the strips. If the weather is warm, you may have to roll the sod in sections as it is laid.

Rolling will also have a leveling effect, but it is better to start with a level sod bed rather than compacting the soil with repeated rolling.

10 Water thoroughly

Improper watering after installation is probably the most common cause of failure in sod lawns. Once the sod has been rolled, water it thoroughly. The soil underneath should be wet to a depth of 6 to 8 inches. From then on, watch it closely. The edges of the sod and pieces along sidewalks and driveways will be the first to dry out, and the last to knit with the soil. They may require spot watering everyday, perhaps more often in hot weather. Make sure the underlying soil is always moist. Once the lawn begins to knit with the soil, you can begin to approach a normal watering schedule (see pages 34 to 39).

Avoid foot traffic, it can slow or damage the establishment of a sod lawn. If this is a problem, cordon the area with stakes, string, and bright flags.

Lawn care

This chapter is designed to simplify lawn care — from mowing and fertilizing to insect, weed, and disease control. Knowing how these aspects interrelate will help you learn how to take better care of your lawn.

After all the what-to-do's and the what-not-to-do's have been outlined in this chapter, it is conceivable that a reader might become overwhelmed with the amount of work involved in caring for a lawn. This conclusion would be unfortunate, since lawn care is entirely up to the lawn owner.

We have presented the plan to grow the perfect lawn, but we also realize that the perfect lawn is not the goal of all people. We provide this information to answer the many questions concerning lawn care. We feel it is important to give you an understanding of how certain aspects of lawn care are interrelated, and how they affect a lawn's appearance.

Level of maintenance
When it comes right down to it, any lawn looks better than having no lawn at all. Take a walk through your neighborhood and observe some of the lawns that look appealing. Notice at the same time how the lawn complements the house. Look closely; is it weed free? . . . are there bad spots? We doubt you'll find many perfect lawns, but lawns aren't required to be perfect, only to be appealing and functional.

The degree of lawn maintenance depends a good deal on convenience and the amount of time one has to spend on lawn care. *When* you fertilize, mow, or take care of weeds, probably depends on when you have the time. These tasks do not have to reduce the pleasure derived from caring for a lawn. Who can say who gets

◁

It's worth it: Everything really does look better with a well-kept lawn.

more enjoyment: the "lawn connoisseur" or the "Saturday morning mower"?

Have a balanced program
Although the different aspects of taking care of a lawn can be broken down conveniently into chapters and subchapters, actual lawn care is not so precise. A lawn that is properly watered and fertilized will have fewer problems with weeds and disease. On the other hand, it will also have to be mowed more often. Regular mowing is a good method of weed control.

The key to success, no matter what your maintenance approach, is to have a balanced program of lawn care. If you mow less, water and fertilize less. If you enjoy getting outdoors and watering, balance this with extra fertilizing.

By understanding all of the needs of your lawn, you will be able to have the lawn you desire. More importantly, you will see that lawn care can be simplified and enjoyable.

A little exercise on a sunny afternoon, the feel and fragrance of a fresh cut lawn — these are the pleasures of lawn care.

Mowing

Notwithstanding pages of magazine cartoons, it's our feeling that most people reading this book don't really mind mowing their lawns. Mowing is a good way to stretch muscles and get out among the neighbors. It's also difficult to imagine anything that smells or feels better than a freshly cut lawn.

Many people who want a handsome lawn don't realize just how important the job of mowing is. A lawn that is mowed when necessary and at the right height resists invasions of weeds, insects, and disease, and has a more lush, healthy look. Mowing infrequently, which often results in removal of too much grass at one time, will eventually produce a lawn with a thin, spotty, or burned out appearance.

How often to mow

How often your lawn needs mowing depends primarily on three things: the kind of grass, how often and how much you water and fertilize, and of greatest importance, the time of year. The best rule of thumb is this: Mow when the grass grows to one-fourth to one-third taller than its recommended mowing height as shown in our chart. In other words, if your lawn's mowing height is 2 inches, mow when it's about 3 inches high, thus removing one-third of the height of the grass blade. Of course, this may not fit your natural, once-a-week habit or allow for vacations. In some cases, it means frequent mowing. For instance, well-fertilized improved bermudagrass in mid-summer may need mowing every two or three days.

The penalty for not following the rule is a stiff one. By letting grass grow too high and then cutting away half or more at once, you expose stems that have been shaded and are not adapted to strong sunlight. Grass leaves may be burned by the sun and turn brown. Mowing too high results in deterioration of green leaf tissue at lower levels. More importantly, roots are severely shocked by a heavy mowing and may need several weeks to recover. Research has shown a direct relationship between height of cut and depth of roots. Roots of grasses properly mowed at correct heights will grow deeper. Deep roots are an important advantage and make lawn care many times easier.

Basically there are two types of mowers ... but with several variations

Power rotary mowers (there are no hand operated rotaries) are popular because of easy maneuverability. They are also easy to adjust for higher cutting and can be used to mow weeds. But they can't go very low and are likely to scalp bumps when set low. They require more power than reel mowers.

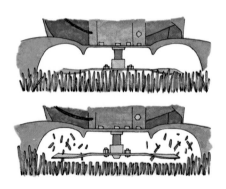

Rotary mowers cut like a spinning scythe. They stand rougher use than reel types. The blades are easy to sharpen, but if they get out of balance the whole mower shakes.

Reel-type mowers give a cleaner, more tailored cut than rotaries, but cannot be operated on high weeds. They do mow lower, making them essential for grasses like improved bermuda and bentgrass. Standard models have four or five blades; models with more blades will cost more, but give a finer cut.

Reel mowers cut with a scissorlike action of spinning blades against a bed knife. They are available in rear and front throw models. Keep the blades sharp —have it done at a mower shop.

The time of year also affects the frequency of mowing. The warm-season grasses commonly used in much of the South barely grow at all in the winter and slowly in the spring and fall. Mowing is infrequent during these times. But during the high temperatures of summer, growth will be more vigorous and mowing will be more frequent.

How much water and fertilizer you apply affects the growth rate of lawns, and consequently, the frequency of mowing. Obviously, lawns maintained at high levels of growth-stimulating fertilizer will require more frequent mowing. For example, golf course greens are usually mowed several times per week, sometimes daily. More labor is one price of the luxurious lawn.

The right height

The proper mowing height depends primarily on the kind of grass. Check the chart on page 51 for the recommended mowing heights of the major lawn grasses. First though, a little theory.

Generally, grasses grow either horizontally or upright. For instance, bermuda and bentgrass spread widely with lateral growing stems called stolons. These stolons parallel the ground as well as the cut of the mower, so are not normally mowed off. Unless grasses like these are kept mowed low, preferably with a heavy reel-type mower, they will in time build-up prodigious amounts of thatch.

Think of it this way. "X" amount of leaf surface is necessary to keep the grass plant healthy and growing. If that leaf surface is spread out low, over a wide area, the lawn can be mowed close to the ground without reducing the necessary leaf surface.

Vertically growing grasses cannot be mowed excessively low since the leaf surface area isn't enough to support the plant. Tall fescue, St. Augustine, bahia, and common Kentucky bluegrass fit into this category. Below a certain height (1½ or 2 inches from the ground), too little leaf surface remains to maintain a good turf.

Mowing too low probably ruins more Kentucky bluegrass lawns than any other practice. This is especially true in transitional areas where adaptation is marginal. Cut high, Kentucky bluegrass is much more disease resistant and can successfully compete

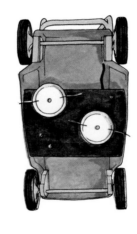

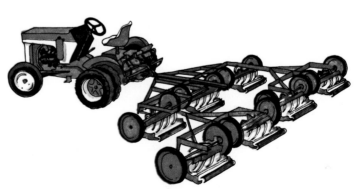

Electric nylon mowers cut grass with nearly the same efficiency as steel-bladed mowers, and are of course much more safe. Two counter-rotating discs powered by separate electric motors spin monofilament line to mow and trim.

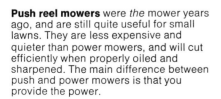

Push reel mowers were *the* mower years ago, and are still quite useful for small lawns. They are less expensive and quieter than power mowers, and will cut efficiently when properly oiled and sharpened. The main difference between push and power mowers is that you provide the power.

Riding mowers and gang mowers (above) are best for lawn areas that are simply too large or time consuming to mow with a conventional reel or rotary. Gang mowers are often used to cut grass at parks and golf course fairways.

with weeds and insects. The tall growth also shades the soil, keeping temperatures lower for cool-loving roots.

Exceptions are some of the new varieties of bluegrass, which are essentially dwarfs. They are more compact and have more leaf surface in less area (see page 16). 'Fylking' and 'Nugget' are two varieties in this category. These dwarfs will tolerate much lower mowing (as low as ¾ inch) than common Kentucky bluegrass.

The University of Georgia points out that the height of a cut can have a big influence on winter survival. Centipedegrass cut at 1½ inches instead of 2½ inches has a much better chance of surviving a winter without damage. St. Augustinegrass is just the opposite; cutting it higher in the fall helps winter survival. This is also true for bermuda, and zoysiagrass, although neither is as susceptible to cold as St. Augustinegrass.

Where shade is a problem, mow another ½ inch higher. This increases the light-trapping power for photosynthesis of the lawn.

The clippings removal question

Some experts say clippings should always be removed, others say it's not necessary. Here's the way the facts sorted out for us.

Latest research has shown that clippings of cool-season grasses left on the lawn do not cause or contribute to thatch. It's the woody, slow-to-decompose stems, rhizomes, and stolons below the grass blades that contribute most to thatch buildup. Clippings of the warm-season zoysiagrass contribute to thatch build-up because they are more stiff and slow to breakdown. How much the clippings of other warm-season grasses contribute to thatch is still an open question.

Clippings return nutrients to the lawn. It's difficult to measure, but some estimates suggest that as much as one-third of a lawn's nitrogen requirement can be supplied by decaying grass clippings.

There are two reasons not to leave clippings on your lawn. First of all, they can be unsightly. Clippings are removed from many a high quality, intensely maintained lawn for just this reason. Secondly, if your lawn is not mowed frequently enough, too much grass will be cut off at one time. Instead of sifting down and decomposing, the clippings can mat on top and suffocate the grass underneath.

At the time of year when your lawn is growing vigorously, clippings will probably have to be removed. With very large lawns, removal of clippings becomes impractical, as is the case with parks and golf courses.

Mowing new lawns

Newly seeded lawns are more delicate than established ones. That's why you have to be more careful mowing them. The soil is very soft and the grass plants usually aren't deeply rooted by the time of the first mowing. On the other hand, mowing young lawns, especially those planted vegetatively, encourages spreading, thus promoting a thicker lawn. Basically, use common sense and apply the same principles of proper mowing of any lawn.

You'll probably want to let the new grass grow a little beyond the normal recommended cutting height. Even then, mow it very lightly, removing less than a third of the total height.

If you can, use a mower that's not too heavy, especially if the soil is still soft. A lightweight rotary or a sharp push-reel mower is your best bet.

If the soil remains too soft or if the new grass is too loosely knit to mow without damage, wait. Let the lawn continue to grow, and then cut it gradually until it is down to the proper height (½ to ¾ inch reduction every second mowing until height is reached).

Lawn mowing miscellany

✓Don't cut wet grass. Why? It can cause uneven mowing, the clippings are messy, and they can mat and suffocate the grass.

✓Pick up stones and sticks before mowing.

✓Alternate mowing patterns. Mowing the same direction every time tends to compact the soil and causes wear patterns.

✓For an attractive "checkered" finish to a lawn, mow it twice, traveling in opposite directions.

✓Reel mowers sometimes cause a ribbed pattern leaving the lawn with a washboard look. This is caused by a mower moving forward too fast for the height of cut. In other words, it's possible to push a mower faster than the blades can make regular cuts.

✓Check blade height with a ruler extended from the cutting edge to a flat surface such as a sidewalk or driveway.

✓Sharp turns with a mower can cause uneven cutting. Make wide turns or use sidewalks and driveways, but be aware of rocks or debris on pavement areas.

✓If the ground is uneven from settling of the soil in some areas, scalping may result as you go over the high spots.

✓Reel mowers are preferred for fine lawns. They cut the grass cleanly, with a scissorlike action and smoothly follow surface contours. They perform

Riding mowers are expensive compared to other mower types, but they can be worth the cost if your lawn area is large.

poorly on tall grasses and lawns with high, wiry seed heads.

✓The blades of rotary mowers are easy to sharpen at home. Only a small portion at the end of the blade actually cuts the grass. Sharpen the edge with a file or grindstone, making sure to even out any rough spots. Check balance before remounting.

✓Flail (also known as hammer knife) and sickle bar are less common types of mowers. Flail mowers use floppy, T-shaped blades revolving on a horizontal shaft to cut grass. They are useful in maintaining rough areas such as vacant lots and the sides of highways. Sickle bar mowers are used for cutting very high grass and weeds. It's the same sort of mower that farmers use to cut field oats and other hays and grains.

✓Experts disagree about the safest way to mow steep inclines. Some say across, others say up and down the slope. Use common sense, and be aware of the danger a power mower represents. Check its stability and be aware that a slipping mower can injure both you and your lawn. Perhaps the best way to handle a slope is to plant a ground cover that doesn't need mowing.

✓Trees in a lawn require special protection from mower damage. See pages 92 and 93.

Lawn mowers

Almost every suburban homeowner has a lawn mower. The number of varieties and styles available proliferates each year. It pays to shop around to see what is available, to find the mower that fits your needs.

The two most common basic mowers are the reel and the rotary. Within each basic type are variations of gas or electric power, walking or riding, push, or self-propelled. Some have bagging attachments, or catchers.

Before buying a lawn mower, look it over carefully. Consider its maneuverability. Make sure the grass catcher is easy to take on and off. Check to see how easy the blades are to adjust. Ask about the safety features. These points will help you choose the right mower.

Mowers can be very specialized. Some are designed to cut high weeds, others are engineered to produce the carpetlike nap of a putting green. There are also the unusual types, such as the one that rides on a cushion of air, and another that cuts with spinning monofilament line.

Reel or rotary: The choice for most people is usually either a rotary mower or a reel. The rotary is by far the most popular. It is generally lower priced, more versatile, and easier to handle and maintain than the reel type.

However, rotary mowers require greater caution in use. They need larger motors with more horsepower, they can never cut as cleanly as a sharp, properly adjusted reel, and few can mow lower than 1 inch.

Reel mowers are available in manual (push) models, or powered with gasoline or electric engines. They cut with a scissor action, which produces the cleanest cut. They conform better to land contours than rotaries, but are impractical on rough, uneven ground or tall-growing grass. They can be adjusted to cut very low, so are the preferred type mower to use for lawns of bermuda or bentgrass, for example.

Power reel mowers discharge clippings from the rear or the front (rear-throw, front-throw). The rear-throw type is widely available and somewhat less expensive. It was most popular before the rotary became the common choice.

Front-throw reel mowers are used primarily by professional landscape gardeners. They are usually well made and can stand contant use. The weight and power of these mowers makes them perfect for the low mowing requirements of tough bermuda or zoysiagrass lawns. Height is also easier to adjust, usually with just a lever. Some can be adjusted low enough to cut right at the soil line.

Riding mowers: You will probably need a riding mower if your lawn is measured in units or multiples of acres. Be aware they are not toys — don't let children play with them. But they are somewhat fun to drive.

Riding mowers cut with the same action as their smaller counterparts — both rotary and reel. Rotaries are the most common.

Mower maintenance

Proper care of your lawn mower will lengthen its lifetime as well as eliminate many time-consuming problems. The manufacturer's maintenance manual for your mower is the best guide. Basically, keep the blades sharp (this is very important) and be sure the motor oil is at the proper level. Clean the mower after use with a soft spray of water. Forceful cleaning with water or air can push dirt into delicate bearings. Do not spray water onto a hot engine.

Keep gaskets and fittings tight; oil or gas dripping onto the lawn will kill the grass.

If you're storing the mower for winter, clean it and drain the gas tank. Come spring, change the oil, clean the spark plug, and refill the gas tank.

Mowing heights

Grass	(inches) Height
Bahiagrass	2-3
Bentgrass	1/4 - 1
Bermudagrass	
Common	1/2 - 1 1/2
Hybrid	1/2 - 1
Bluegrass	
Common	2-3
Improved (varies by variety)	3/4 - 2 1/2
Buffalograss	1-3
Carpetgrass	1-2
Centipedegrass	1-2
Dichondra	1/2 - 1 1/2
Fescue	
Chewing	1-2
Red	2-3
Tall	3-4
Annual ryegrass	1 1/2 - 2
Perennial ryegrass	1 - 2 1/2
St. Augustinegrass	1 - 2 1/2
Zoysiagrass	1/2 - 1 1/2

Safety tips

Power lawn mowing equipment is so common it is taken for granted. But power mowers alone are responsible for thousands of accidents yearly. Follow the guidelines below and those of the mower manufacturer, and you'll miss becoming an injury statistic.

Don't disconnect manufacturer's safety features and always keep in mind the possible dangers.

Many fingers have been lost unclogging discharge chutes of rotary mowers. Make a habit of turning off the power and disconnecting the spark plug before thinking about reaching into the clogged grass.

Don't try to mow where the terrain is too steep or uneven. Again, many accidents have occurred on slippery, steep slopes.

Walk over a lawn area before mowing and look for rocks, toys, sprinkler heads, and other possible obstructions.

Don't allow children to mow until they are strong and mature enough to handle the job.

The why, how, and when of fertilization

Lawn owners accept the fact that they must mow and water to be able to maintain their lawn's health. Some may question the need for fertilizer, but they shouldn't.

Lawngrasses live in what is basically an unnatural environment. They are crowded together and compete with each other, as well as neighboring trees and shrubs, for water and nutrients. They are mowed regularly and their clippings often removed.

Because of this competition and the unnatural demands placed on lawns, they must be fertilized. Just as a balanced diet works best for people and animals, the same is true of lawns — they need fertilizer for sustenance. Properly fertilized, the lawn will maintain good color, density, and vigor and will not easily succumb to insects, weeds, or diseases. Underfertilized, the lawn is not only less attractive, but is considerably more susceptible to environmental stress and damage.

The nutrients a lawn needs

Scientists have singled out 16 different mineral elements as essential to the growth of all plants. Some are very common, such as oxygen from air and hydrogen from water. Others, such as zinc or boron, are needed in only minute amounts usually found naturally in most soils.

Nitrogen is by far the most important element needed by a lawn. It promotes rapid growth and gives lawns a healthy color. It is also the one most often in short supply. Watering flushes it from the soil and the growing plant needs a plentiful and continuous supply. Without sufficient nitrogen, growth stops and the lawn becomes pale and yellowish.

Phosphorus is the next most important element needed for healthy growth of lawn grasses. It is required to produce strong root growth. Phosphorus stimulates early root formation, particularly essential to the proper development of new plantings. It is not readily flushed from the soil by watering and is needed by grass in small quantities, so most balanced lawn fertilizers contain only a low percentage.

Potassium is the third element of critical importance. Like nitrogen, it is flushed out by water but at a much slower rate. It is very important to the hardiness and disease resistance of lawn grasses, and helps promote wearability. Potassium is needed in about the same quantity as nitrogen but soil minerals supply a considerable amount, therefore, not as much is added to fertilizers.

Calcium, sulfur and magnesium are also needed in relatively large amounts. Calcium is either present in adequate quantities in the soil or is added through periodic applications of lime. Dolomite (or dolomitic limestone) supplies magnesium as well as calcium. Most sulfur reaches a lawn through the air, water, or organic matter.

Micronutrients are elements needed in small amounts. If your lawn does not green-up with an application of nitrogen, the problem may be a shortage of iron. This is particularly true in areas where soil pH is high. (Yellowing can also be caused from sulfur deficiency, over-watering, manganese deficiency in sandy soils, and a pH less than 5.) A soil test may help solve persistent, seemingly soil-related problems such as these.

Types of fertilizers

A little garden store shopping will reveal an abundance of lawn fertilizers. You'll see labels proclaiming "fast-acting," "slow-release," "organic" and so on. But if they all contain the same basic minerals, which they do, what's the difference? Here is a description of these products.

Organic. A chemist might argue that some man-made fertilizers are technically "organic." Here organic refers to a fertilizer derived from plant or animal waste.

The variety of organic fertilizers is endless. There are manures of all kinds — municipal sewage sludge, blood meals, and seed meals. They all share some advantages and some disadvantages. In some areas, they may be inexpensive and easy to obtain, yet the reverse is often true. Most have distinctly beneficial soil building properties covered in more detail on pages 27 to 31.

Usually the action of organics is slow, making it difficult to make a mistake and overfertilize. This is the major difference of organic fertilizers compared to synthetic fertilizers — nutrients are slowly released. (Bloodmeal is an exception. It is a fast release organic, almost as fast as mineral fertilizers.)

Organics are bulkier, heavier, and more difficult to handle. They have a low percentage of nitrogen so it is necessary to apply a much greater quantity at one time. (They may also be unpleasant to the nose.)

The main disadvantage of organic fertilizers is that the timing of nutrient release is not predictable. This is because soil microbes must be actively digesting the material making the nutrients it contains available to the lawn. Because microbes are most active when the soil is warmest, much of the organic carrier's nutrient is made available during warm weather which, as stated elsewhere, is not the best time for a lawn to receive a heavy fertilization.

Soluble synthetic: These are the most common fertilizers used on lawns today. They too have advantages and disadvantages.

The big advantage of this type of fertilizer is predictability. Because their characteristics are known precisely, you know exactly the effect they will have on the lawn. For many types of lawns this is an important feature. They are available to the lawn before the soil has thoroughly warmed in summer, they are lower in cost than organic fertilizers, and easier to handle. Less material need be applied since the percentage of nitrogen is usually high.

There may be more work required of the gardener who uses these. More applications are necessary because the effects are short term. If your lawn requires 8 pounds of actual nitrogen a year, almost that many separate applications will be necessary.

Further, there is the possibility of "fertilizer burn" if overapplied, if the lawn is wet as you spread the fertilizer, or if the fertilizer is not thoroughly watered in after application.

The exceptions are some "weed and feed" products which are formulated with soluble fertilizers and are designed for use on wet grass (when temperatures are moderate — under 85°.

Slow release: To some extent these fertilizers combine the characteristics of the organics and soluble synthetics. Usually they have a high percentage of nitrogen so handling large quantities of material is not necessary. But the possibility of fertilizer burn is highly reduced since the nitrogen does not become available to the plant all at once.

There are a variety of types, but most are categorized on a fertilizer bag under the heading "W.I.N.," meaning water insoluble nitrogen. Many of the commonly available lawn fertilizers are actually a combination of soluble nitrogen and W.I.N. nitrogen.

Slow release fertilizers are favored by many lawn growers because they make heavier applications of nitrogen possible, hence fewer applications are necessary. However, they don't provide a quick green-up. You will not have the degree of control of greening response that's possible with soluble synthetics, but will have slightly more than with organics.

Percentage W.I.N.

In order to determine the actual percentage of water insoluble nitrogen (W.I.N.), it's necessary to do a little arithmetic. For example, if you have a 25-3-7 fertilizer with 7.6% W.I.N., multiply the 7.6 by 100 equalling 760. Divide the 760 by the total percentage nitrogen shown on the bag. In this case 760 divided by 25 equals 30.4 Thus 30.4% of the nitrogen is W.I.N.

Lawn experts have determined that fertilizers less than 15% W.I.N. are basically fast acting. Between 15 and 30% is medium and any more than 30% insoluble is a slow release fertilizer. A slow-release fertilizer is less likely to burn the lawn after application and is less subject to being flushed from the soil by water.

Use a complete fertilizer

A complete fertilizer is one that contains all three of the primary nutrients: nitrogen, phosphate, and potash. Every state requires that the percentages of these three elements be prominently displayed on every bag of fertilizer. Always, the first number is nitrogen, the second phoshate, and the third potassium. An example is 24-4-8. These numbers state the percentages of nutrients in the bag compared to the total contents of the bag.

As a general guide, a 3 to 1 to 2 ratio of nutrients has proven to be good for home lawn fertilization. However, factors such as local climate, soil conditions, and the form of nitrogen in the fertilizer can influence what's best in various localities.

A 3 to 1 to 2 fertilizer could have a formula of 21-7-14. It is not critical for a fertilizer to be exactly this ratio, but something close to it is recommended. For instance, a higher nitrogen ratio of 6 to 1 to 2 (formula 24-4-8) is common.

Generally this ratio of nutrients is properly applied by using the products of a lawn food manufacturer in a label-directed way. There are general purpose types as well as those designed for specific grasses.

These ratios are based on the demand of the growing lawn for these nutrients. Usually a lawn needs three to five times as much nitrogen as phosphorus and two times as much potassium as phosphorus. (Although nitrogen and potassium are needed by the plant in similar amounts, some nitrogen is flushed from the soil by water and is lost.)

Reading a fertilizer label

All manufacturers supply the same basic information on a lawn food label. Plant food control agencies and state laws stipulate the specific information that must appear on a label. There will be differences, but the most important characteristics, described below, are found on every bag of fertilizer sold as lawn food.

Lawn Food: In this example, "Lawn Food" is the equivalent of a brand name.

Guaranteed Analysis: The manufacturers' warranty that the stated analysis at least is present in the container. The guaranteed analysis is always stated in this order and form.

Sources of nitrogen: These percentages are not required in every case but most manufacturers normally supply this information. Nitrogen sources have different characteristics (see Ortho's *All About Fertilizers, Soils & Water*) so it is useful to know which ones are used in the fertilizer you buy. This percentage W.I.N. indicates this fertilizer is medium to slow acting (see page 53).

24-4-8: Referred to as formula grade, or analysis, these numbers are the percentage of nitrogen, phosphate, and potash (in that order) of the contents.

Available phosphoric acid/soluble potash: These percentages are listed only if their presence is claimed. The actual of this fertilizer is 6 to 1 to 2.

Primary nutrients: The more basic fertilizers from which this product is made.

Potential acidity: This fertilizer has a slightly acidifying action Calcium carbonate is laboratory quality ground limestone. About 8 pounds of ground limestone would completely neutralize the potential acidity of this 20 pounds.

Lawn Food 24-4-8

Guaranteed Analysis:

Total Nitrogen (N) 24%

    4.1% Ammoniacal Nitrogen
    15.9% Urea Nitrogen
    4.0% Water Insoluble Nitrogen

Available Phosphoric Acid (P_2O_5) 4%

Soluble Potash (K_2O) 8%

    Primary Nutrients from Urea, Ureaform, Ammonium Sulfate, Ammonium Phosphate, and Muriate of Potash.

Potential Acidity 800 lbs. Calcium Carbonate Equivalent per ton. Net Weight 20 lbs.

Liquid fertilizers are applied by hand-held hose-attached sprayers. Some operators may have trouble applying spray evenly.

Spreading fertilizer by hand requires a talented touch. An underhand swing, as above, provides the best results.

Drop spreaders are very useful on small lawns. Make sure you overlap applications just enough so that no strips are left unfed.

Actual nitrogen

The amount of "actual" nitrogen is a term we have used throughout this book. It is simply a convenient way to say how much fertilizer a lawn should receive, without figuring the specific type or formula of lawn fertilizer you might use. For example, a 100 pound bag of 24-4-8 (24 percent nitrogen) contains 24 pounds of actual nitrogen. A 20 pound bag of 24-4-8 contains 4.8 pounds of actual nitrogen (20 pounds multiplied by .24 equals 4.8 pounds).

If you want to apply 1 pound of actual nitrogen over 1,000 square feet of lawn using this 24-4-8 fertilizer, you would use 4.17 pounds.

The directions on the bag will usually provide instructions as to the proper amount to use. Most labeled instructions follow the basic guideline of recommending application rates that supply approximately one pound of actual nitrogen per 1,000 square feet. There are exceptions; fertilizers with high percentages of W.I.N. or slow release forms of nitrogen are often applied at higher rates.

Fertilizer and pesticide combinations

In recent years, many combinations of pesticides and fertilizers have become available. Common types contain herbicides for broadleaf weed control or preemergence herbicides for crabgrass control. There are also products that include other pesticides for insect and disease control.

These products do have definite advantages. Considerable time, labor, and equipment are saved if two jobs can be accomplished in one. Less total material is handled and less storage space is required. In addition, the cost of the combined material may be less than the cost of the individual ingredients purchased separately. Most important, the pesticide can often be applied more evenly and closer to the recommended rate than if it was sprayed on the lawn.

The disadvantage of these kinds of products is the difficulty in making applications at the proper time, since the best time to fertilize is not always the best time to control insects or weeds. Be certain the growth cycles of the insects and weeds coincide with combination product applications for best results. A fertilizer combined with a pesticide is most useful if the advantages and limitations are understood.

When to fertilize

Few gardeners need to be reminded to feed their lawns in spring. It helps a lawn get a head start on pests, weeds, and the summer heat that's soon to come.

By midsummer, heat and light intensity slow down the growth of the cool-season grasses. They usually remain green but are essentially dormant. We recommend, with only a few exceptions, no feeding of the cool-season grasses in mid-summer.

The most important time to fertilize cool-season grasses is in fall. Fall fertilization keeps the grass growing green and longer into cold weather. The lawn is stimulated to become more dense. Fall feeding also gives the lawn a chance to store food that will get it off to a fast start next spring. Not much top growth takes place in fall so a lawn can store food that will get it off to a fast start next spring.

Growth of the warm-season grasses peaks in midsummer then tapers off in fall, continuing at a slower pace until frost. The first sign of spring green comes when the soil is still cold. This is the time when lawn food with quick-acting forms of nitrogen pays off, making grass fully green sooner.

Warm-season grasses can also benefit from fall fertilization, with two exceptions. If winter weeds are a problem, their growth will be further stimulated by the feeding.

A heavy fertilization may also promote a flush of succulent growth that, in some areas, leaves the grass more susceptible to cold injury. Otherwise, fall fertilization will keep the grass green and growing longer in the fall and promote earlier spring green-up.

Lime

In areas of the country with heavy rainfall, soils are typically acid. Grasses grow poorly in highly acid soils because of nutrient imbalance and toxicity. Acid soil is corrected by adding lime.

Hand-held broadcast spreaders operate by turning a side-arm crank; the fertilizer flies out from a whirling wheel.

Push-type broadcast spreaders are ideal for large lawns. Before using, measure the "throw" to avoid uneven applications.

a wide area via a whirling wheel. Because they require fewer passes to completely cover the lawn, they are easier to use, especially on large lawns. Make sure you measure the throw width so you know how far to space your passes. This can be easily determined by running the spreader over dark-colored pavement for a short distance. (Note: some overlap is necessary for uniform coverage.)

Spreader settings: Push-type drop and broadcast spreaders usually have adjustable settings which correspond to application rates on fertilizer bags. Although fairly accurate when the spreaders are new, they should be calibrated (the actual application rate tested) at least once a year. Instructions for doing this are on page 96 of this book. Hand-held broadcast spreaders can be calibrated the same way.

Drop-type fertilizer spreaders are also used to spread seed. Calibration is again necessary to make sure you apply appropriate quantities of seed.

Application: The best technique for applying lawn food is to cover the ends of the lawn first, then go back and forth the long way. To avoid double applications, make sure to shut off the spreader as you approach the end strips. Keep the spreader closed while you are turning around, backing up, or stopped. For even and thorough coverage, walk at normal speed and keep the spreader level.

If you do happen to spill or drop extra dry fertilizer in one area, it should be scraped or vacuumed up. The area should then be flooded with water to avoid fertilizer burn.

After fertilizing, brush or wash out the spreader immediately after use to avoid corrosion. Dry thoroughly before storing.

The only sure way to know if your lawn needs lime is through a soil test. However, liming is a way of life in many areas. In those areas, you already know your soil needs lime.

Soil acidity is measured by its pH. On a scale of 14, pH 7 is neutral, above 7 is alkaline, and below 7 is acid. If your soil pH is below 5.5, lime is necessary. A soil pH between 5.5 and 7.5 is good for most grasses and 6.8 to 7 is ideal. (Centipedegrass is an important exception: it prefers more acid soil. Add lime if pH is below 4.5 enough to raise pH to 6.)

The easiest and best form of lime for lawns is ground limestone. Your soil test will provide recommended rates. Lime is best applied with a mechanical spreader.

How to apply fertilizer

The five basic methods of applying fertilizers are shown in the photographs on these pages.

Liquid fertilizers are applied by hand-held or hose-attached sprayers. Their basic faults are difficulty in applying the fertilizer evenly, frequent fills, and the amount of time it takes to apply adequate amounts. Read the directions on both the liquid fertilizer and the sprayer carefully. Rates are set up according to ratios of liquid fertilizer and water added to the sprayer. Also make sure all parts of the sprayer are attached and operational.

You can broadcast dry fertilizer by hand, but it requires a talented touch to be efficient. It often causes uneven streaking in the lawn. Use this method only in very small areas or if there is no other alternative.

The use of a drop sreader is a very common method to apply a dry fertilizer. It requires more passes than a broadcast spreader, and is most useful on a medium-sized lawn. When using a drop spreader, overlap the wheels enough so no strips are left underfed, but also be careful not to double feed any sections. If this happens, you'll have uneven greening in the lawn, or worse, fertilizer burn.

The use of a broadcast spreader is probably the easiest way of applying a dry fertilizer. There are two types — hand-held and push-wheel models. Each throws the fertilizer pellets over

Nitrogen requirements

Pounds of nitrogen per year	Warm-season	Cool-season
1 to 3	Carpetgrass Centipedegrass	Hard fescue
2 to 4	—	Red fescue Chewings fescue Kentucky bluegrass (common)
4 to 6	Bahiagrass St. Augustinegrass Zoysiagrass	Tall fescue Annual ryegrass Colonial bentgrass Perennial ryegrass
6 to 12	Bermudagrasses Dichondra	Kentucky bluegrass (improved) Creeping bentgrass

These rates show the range for grasses with a long growing season. Lower rates would apply to northern and eastern areas with short seasons.

Lawn renovation

If your lawn deteriorates to the point that routine cultural practices such as mowing, fertilization, watering, and weed control, do not give the desired response, it is probably time to renovate. By renovating, it is possible to renew your lawn without going to the trouble of completely rebuilding the lawn.

The University of Arkansas says: "Maybe you are wondering whether to destroy your old lawn and establish a new one or to renovate the old lawn.

"Many factors can cause a poor lawn. Lack of adequate fertilizer is most common. Other problems such as mowing too low, lack of weed control, frequent light watering, shade, thatch, low soil pH, buried rocks or debris, drought-prone steep banks, wet soils, foot paths, diseases and insects — all contribute to a poor-quality lawn. Usually an analysis of the problems and solutions suggests that it would be easier to correct specific problems and apply a good cultural program to the existing lawn."

Renovation may involve the use of heavy equipment available from a rental yard (see page 57). There are many lawn service companies that specialize in these kinds of services. In any case, renovation is a chance to improve the overall quality of your lawn.

Thatch

If you need to renovate your lawn because of thatch build-up, you have a lot of company. The spongy feel to lawns with heavy thatch is a result of a thick layer of slowly decomposing stems, roots, and debris. A thin layer of thatch, ¼ to ½ inch, may actually be beneficial because it buffers soil temperature and adds to the lawn's resilience. This reduces the compaction of soil that results from heavy use.

If thick enough, thatch can actually be water repellent or "hydrophopic." A conscientious waterer may think he or she is watering enough, but actually the water never reaches the soil. Grass roots that grow in the thatch layer instead of the soil are naturally less drought resistant, since the moisture in the thatch evaporates much faster.

Insects and disease find thatch a particularly suitable place to inhabit. Since water cannot penetrate, neither can pest control materials.

Finally, variable thickness and density of thatch makes scalping by mowers almost inevitable. Dethatching of Southern grasses is best done in spring just prior to spring greenup.

Why thatch accumulates: Thatch accumulates fastest in lawns composed of spreading type grasses. Notorious thatch builders include warm-season grasses such as bermuda and zoysiagrass. In temperate climates the bentgrasses and 'Merion' bluegrass are the worst. Dwarf-type bluegrasses also build up thatch.

What to do about thatch: Soil penetrants, or wetting agents, only reduce the symptoms of thatch. They counteract its hydrophopic character, but the effect is shortlived and definitely not a cure. Bacterial agents that supposedly breakdown thatch have also proven to be ineffective.

There are attachments for rotary mowers that may be helpful in thatch removal. A thatch hand rake that has knifelike blades instead of the usual hard steel teeth can be used. As a last resort, a sod cutter can remove especially thick thatch if it has built up to impossible levels. (Note: this is only applicable for grasses that have underground runners.) Adjust the sod cutter to cut just above the soil level instead of below. Fixed, flail, and spring-tooth mowers are also available for dethatching.

The Mississippi State Extension says: "The most accepted way to dethatch a home lawn is by vertical mowing. The vertical mower is a specialized machine that thins the grass and brings much of the thatch to the surface of the lawn. You then sweep, rake, or vacuum this material from the lawn."

The University of Florida adds: "The blades of vertical mowers should be spaced differently for different grasses. Berumda and zoysiagrass can stand heavy thinning. Space blades only 1 inch apart. Centipedegrass should be less severely thinned. Space blades 1½ to 2 inches apart. Bahia and St. Augustinegrass should be the least thinned. Space blades 3 inches apart.

"Zoysia and bermudagrass can be vertically mowed close to soil level in several directions without damage. Bahia, centipede, and St. Augustinegrass should not be vertically mowed closer than 1 inch from the ground. They do not have the recuperative powers of zoysia and bermudagrass." Otherwise, the depth of penetration of the blade should be adjusted so that the blades will completely penetrate

The easiest way to repair a damaged section of lawn is to patch it with a piece of sod custom cut to fit the area.

through the thatch layer and into the soil under the thatch.

These recommendations are valuable for realizing the recuperative powers of different grasses, but adjusting blades on a vertical mower is usually difficult. If you rent one it is probably impossible. Make only one pass on a slow-to-recover grass if you cannot properly adjust the blades.

Dethatch timing: The best time to dethatch is just before the lawn's most vigorous growth of the season. For warm-season grasses, dethatching should be done with the beginning of warm weather in late spring. Cool-season grasses grow best in spring and fall. The prime time to dethatch is in the fall; the second best time is early spring.

About aeration

Roots need air as well as water and nutrients for growth. Lawns, especially those that receive heavy use, can develop compacted, air-deficient soil. Compacted soil also restricts water absorption. A foot-path worn into a lawn is compaction. To correct the many problems of compacted soil, lawn professionals have developed specialized tools and techniques.

Correcting compacted soil is described by a variety of names, including "hole punching," "coring," and "aerification." All are based on the same principle: Hollow metal tubes ¼ to ¾ inch in diameter are pushed into the soil by foot or machine, to a depth of 3 to 4 inches, sometimes deeper. The soil should be *moist* when doing this, not too wet, not too dry.

Take a look at the photographs (next page) of the aerifier used on one of our lawns.

Overseeding in winter

The only disadvantage of the warm-season grasses is their winter dormancy. Scientists say that it is caused by a combination of low temperatures and winter sunlight. Whatever the cause, most lawn owners prefer all-year green color. Lawns can either be painted green or overseeded (see "lawn tips," page 92 to 93).

Grasses for overseeding: Annual ryegrass is suitable for overseeding dormant bermudagrass. The seed is inexpensive and widely available. Use it heavily: about 10 pounds per 1,000 square feet.

Turf-type perennial ryegrass is excellent for overseeding. The color is a dark green and the growth rate is slower than that of annual ryegrass, resulting in less mowing.

The fine fescues are also good for overseeding. Use them alone or in combination with the ryegrasses.

To be successful in overseeding, close mowing, dethatching, and (if possible) aerification are recommended. These steps help ensure close contact of seed and soil. As an alternative, mow close to the soil with a heavy, reel-type mower. Seed, and finish with a top dressing of peat moss or similar organic material. Don't forget to water frequently until the new grass is firmly rooted into the soil.

The following spring, encourage the growth of the permanent lawn grass at the expense of the winter cover. Just before the late spring flush of growth, vertical mow again or mow close and fertilize. This will be enough of a shock to the winter cover and enough of a boost to the main lawngrass to reestablish.

Patching

Patching involves removing the weedy, dead, or damaged section of the lawn and replacing it with a piece of sod or by reseeding. It is always done with the same variety of grass as the present lawn. Many nurseries nor-mally stock a small amount of sod just for this purpose.

Dig out the damaged area and loosen the soil underneath. If spilled gasoline or herbicide is the cause of the dead spot, remove several inches of the soil and replace it. Bring the underlying soil to proper grade and cut a piece of sod to fit.

Of course, patching can be done with seed, too. The process is the same as with any new seeding. Regardless of the method, remember to give close attention to watering for several weeks.

A renovating experience

On the following two pages we show the steps we took to renovate one of our lawns. We chose seed rather than sod to get the full growing experience.

The lawn had many weeds, including unwanted bermudagrass and oxalis, requiring the most drastic kind of renovation. The entire lawn area was sprayed with a systemic herbicide, glyphosate. One week later we dethatched, aerified, and seeded.

A trip to a rental yard near Santa Rosa, California, produced the photograph of lawn equipment for rent. Moving clockwise from the upper left corner is a sickle or bar mower **(a)**. *They are perfect for that empty lot overgrown with weeds. A high-wheel rotary mower* **(b)** *cuts higher than most rotaries — about 4 inches — and is much easier to maneuver over rough terrain. A sod cutter* **(c)** *can be useful two ways. One, you can strip off old turf, or two, remove thatch. Riding mowers* **(d)** *are perfect for big, relatively smooth lawns. The type pictured has a rotary mower mounted midsection. Lawn aerators,* **(e)** *are used to remove cores of soil. This provides air in the grass root zone. As soil becomes compacted, the amount of air space in the soil is reduced. A vertical mower* **(f)** *goes by at least two other names: dethatcher or lawn comb. This piece of equipment cuts perpendicular to the surface of the lawn, slicing deep into thatch. After one pass it's easy to rake up the thatch debris. Two types of edgers, power and manual, are pictured* **(g)**. *Hand edgers are fine for most trimming needs. Power types are an advantage for large lawns. The two lawn rollers* **(h)** *may look similar but have completely different uses. The barrel type is filled with water to reduce the fluffiness of freshly rototilled soil. and to provide good contact between seed or sod and the soil. (Use it half or less than half full.) The other roller is used to spread bulky organic topdressing materials such as peat moss, manure, or composted bark. It is shown in action on page 27. Besides vertical mowers and riding mowers, most rental yards will have a variety of common lawn mower types* **(i)** . *You can rent a heavy reel mower for the one or two times you need to cut the lawn extra low for thatch removal.*

Remove undesirable weeds and grasses 1

The lawn at the right contained bermudagrass as well as various broadleaf weeds. The entire lawn was killed using glyphosate. Herbicides, such as 2-4, D, are chemicals that would be used if the lawn was infested with broadleaf weeds. Always read labels carefully when using herbicides. Be sure materials are safe to use around trees and shrubs. Never use pre-emergent weed controls, unless specifically recommended, prior to reseeding. Make sure the chemical leaves no residue that may harm young grasses.

Using a vertical mower, verticut the existing lawn 2

In order to have contact between seed and soil, it is necessary to remove as much thatch as possible. Vertical mowers remove thatch like mechanical rakes, slicing vertically into the soil with knives or tines. Notice the grooves that the vertical mower leaves in the soil. Use the vertical mower on a damp lawn, never dry or soaking wet. For the best results, go over the lawn twice in opposite directions.

Low mowing and vigorous raking with a steel rake may be sufficient to remove thatch from small lawns. However, it is a tedious process and much less efficient than a vertical mower. Dethatching attachments are also available for rotary mowers, but these are not as thorough.

Rake up debris 3

Thoroughly rake up any loose debris left by vertical mowing. (There can be quite a lot.) This guarantees the all-important contact between seed and soil. The debris should be discarded if chemicals were used previously. Otherwise, the dead grass and thatch removed by vertical mowing make an excellent addition to the compost pile or as a mulch for the vegetable garden.

4 Aerate the soil

Aerators remove small cores of soil from the lawn which allows air, water, and nutrients to pass freely to the roots. Aeration is best done on a damp lawn. Remove the soil cores by raking, or shred with a rotary mower, and use them to level any uneven spots.

This lawn had several low spots that made mowing difficult. If there are high and low spots in the new seed-bed, add a good topsoil or peatmoss and sand, and level with a rake. It may be necessary to flatten high spots with a steel rake. If crushed soil cores left over from aeration are used for leveling, it may be desirable to blend them with additional organic matter.

5 Add lime, fertilize, and sow seed

If liming is a way of life in your area, this is the time to do it. It's also the time to apply a complete balanced fertilizer.

If a good percentage of desirable grasses are present, it may not be necessary to reseed, just fertilize and water heavily. If you do seed or use vegetative methods to re-establish, follow a good watering program.

Right after planting is a critical time in the re-establishment of healthy turf. It may be necessary to water several times a day in hot weather in order to keep the seed, sprigs, or stolons moist until they become established.

6 The end result, a renovated lawn

This photograph was taken just six weeks after the renovation process was completed. It's important to stress, however, that lawn care doesn't end here. In order to keep problems from re-occurring and to keep the lawn looking its best, you need to follow an efficient program of fertilization, watering, mowing, and dethatching.

Lawn weeds

Weeds are simply plants in the wrong place. The finest lawngrass plant is a weed in the vegetable garden and, likewise, dandelions are cultivated in some of the best vegetable gardens.

Most lawn weeds are easily eliminated. Mowing at the right height, fertilizing adequately, and good watering practices will go a long way in achieving a weed-free lawn.

A healthy lawn will not be troubled much by weeds. Since problems and questions do come up, we've put together the following short course on weeds. The following five pages contain photographs of the most common lawn weeds, and their controls.

First, some definitions

Annual: A plant that lives only one year.

Perennial: A plant that lives for two or more years.

Herbicide: A chemical used to kill plants.

Pre-emergence: A term used to describe herbicides that are effective against germinating seeds — before the plant emerges through the soil surface.

Post-emergence: A term used to describe herbicides that are effective after a plant breaks through the soil surface.

Contact herbicide: Kills plant parts covered by the spray. Affects only above-ground parts.

Systemic herbicide: Absorbed by the plant to circulate inside it, killing all parts, including the roots.

How weeds get in the lawn

Weed seeds are in most soils by the millions. They wait, dormant, until brought to the soil surface or until the lawngrass dies, when light and moisture start them growing. Some seeds can remain alive in the soil for many years. That is why some weed treatments are useful before you plant.

How to control lawn weeds

The more weeds you eliminate before planting will naturally leave fewer to battle later on. Following is one of the best methods of weed elimination. Simply keep the soil bare and moist for three or four months, and either till, or spray with a contact herbicide every three weeks, as the weed seeds germinate. If it's awkward to leave your soil bare that long, try another method.

Fumigation is another pre-plant weed treatment. It too, usually involves time — at least three weeks. (Check the label directions.) Vapam makes a gas that kills many weed seeds and other soil organisms. It works very well, but is neither inexpensive or simple to apply. Also, it may harm nearby tree or shrub roots if roots extend into the treated area. Methyl bromide is another soil fumigant which works well and is fast (two to three days), but it is the most dangerous one to use, so much so, we don't recommend it for home lawns, unless used by a professional. A special permit is usually required. The only other pre-plant weed control method is the use of a pre-emergence herbicide. Some types will discriminate between the weed and the lawn grass seed; one is Tupersan.

Weed killers

Weeds are of two types: broadleaf or narrowleaf. Broadleaf weeds have more obvious, showy flowers. Their leaves have a network of small veins originating from a principal point or vein which divides the leaf in half. Dandelion and Carolina geranium are typical broadleaf weeds.

Narrowleaf weeds are the grasses. They usually have hollow stems and long, narrow leaf blades with parallel veins. Dallisgrass and crabgrass are common narrowleaf weeds.

Another weed type, much less common, are the sedges. They look similar to grasses, but have triangular stems. It is important to stress the differences between these weed types. An herbicide that kills one type may not even affect the other. Also, it is particularly important to pay strict attention to labeled instructions. Many weed killers or pest controls are only effective within certain temperature ranges and stages of plant maturity. Be very careful when applying any chemical products. Don't spray on windy days, and keep children away when you do spray.

Weed killers are either pre-emergent or post-emergent. The post-emergent types are further categorized as either contact or systemic. Chemical names are listed first. Trade names follow in parenthesis.

Pre-emergents

Benefin (Balan). Controls annual grasses in most lawns. Don't use on bentgrass. It will prevent all seeds from germinating for up to eight weeks.

Bensulide (Betasan). Another control for annual grasses and certain broad-leaves. Don't try to reseed for four months after application.

DCPA (Dacthal). Especially effective on germinating grasses and seed of certain broadleaf species, including chickweed and purslane. Don't use on new lawns and don't reseed for 10 to 12 weeks after using.

Siduron (Tupersan). Effectively controls weedy grasses such as crab grass, foxtail, and barnyard grass. It has the unique quality of not interfering with the germination of cool-season grasses such as Kentucky bluegrass.

Post-emergents

Cacodylic acid (Contax, Phytar-560). Kills only upon contact. Very effective although repeat treatments are necessary before it will kill tough perennials such as bermudagrass. Kills all green-growing leaf tissue, does not move within plants to roots. Often used to clear lawns of existing growth, prior to renovation.

2,4-D. Widely available in many forms and products. It is essentially a growth-influencing hormone that singles out the broadleaf weeds in the lawn, killing them, without damaging most lawn grasses.

MCPP (Mecoprop). Related and very similar to 2,4-D but safer to use on new lawns or sensitive grasses such as bentgrass or St. Augustinegrass.

Dicamba (Banvel). Particularly effective against clover, beggarweed, chickweed, knotweed, and red sorrel. It is a hormone-type weed killer as 2,4-D but is taken up through roots as well as through leaves. Be very careful using it around trees and shrubs or in areas where roots underlay the area to be treated.

Dalapon (Dowpon). Effective against all grasses. Usually used for spot treatment of undesired clumps of bermudagrass or tall fescue. Use in the West to eliminate bermudagrass from dichondra lawns. Use carefully, excessive rates can damage dichondra.

DSMA, MSMA, MAMA (available in many combinations under several trade names). Used to control grassy weeds such as crabgrass and foxtail. They kill mostly by foliage activity. Effective against hard-to-kill nutsedges.

Glyphosate (Roundup). Non-selective and systemic: It will kill both grasses and broadleaf weeds. It is the best herbicide for control of bermudagrass, and is also useful against other perennial grassy weeds.

Annual bluegrass or **Poa annua.** Narrowleaf. Annual.

Season of fast growth: Prefers cool weather of spring and fall. Tends to die out in summer.

Pre-emergence control: DCPA, bensulide, and benefin. Apply in early August. Several applications may be necessary.

Post-emergence control: None.

Bermudagrass, devilgrass. Narrowleaf. Perennial.

Season of fast growth: Summer. Grows fast when temperatures are high.

Pre-emergence control: None.

Post-emergence control: Dalapon is one of the best. The newer glyphosate will also control bermudagrass but may be hard to find in most areas.

Comments: Where bermudagrass is well adapted to the climate, *it is your lawn* or a troublesome weed.

Crabgrass. Narrowleaf. Annual.

Season of fast growth: A summer weed. Begins in early spring and grows fast until seed heads form in late summer to fall.

Pre-emergence control: Products containing DCPA, benefin, bensulide, and siduron. Weed killer must be applied in spring before seedlings appear. Check "Lawns in your area," pages 80 to 89, and "Lawn calendar," pages 92 to 93.

Post-emergence control: DSMA, MSMA, MAMA. Apply when weeds are small and much easier to control. One or more repeat treatments at 7- to 10-day intervals may be necessary.

Dallisgrass. Narrowleaf. Perennial.

Season of fast growth: Dallisgrass is a summer weed, but will grow all year in mild climates.

Pre-emergence control: None.

Post-emergence control: Use DSMA, MAMA, or MSMA every ten days or as the label directs as a spot spray. Check label before using on St. Augustine, centipede or bahiagrass.

Comments: Thrives in low wet areas. Try to drain the soil first for control. Bahiagrass is a close relative and sometimes infests bermudagrass lawns. Similar treatment will control.

Dandelion. Broadleaf. Perennial.

Season of fast growth: Spring and fall.

Pre-emergence control: None.

Post-emergence control: Sprays containing 2,4-D or mecoprop are very effective. Apply during spring or fall when growth is active, but before yellow flowers appear. Spray or treat on a windless day when temperatures are above 60°F. but less than 80°F.

Comments: Improved turf varieties usually resist dandelion invasion quite well.

Dock. Broadleaf. Perennial.

Season of fast growth: Spring and fall.

Pre-emergence control: None.

Post-emergence control: Use 2, 4-D, mecoprop, or dicamba mid-spring or mid-fall.

English daisy. Broadleaf. Perennial.

Season of fast growth: Cool weather of spring and fall. All season if protected from drought and high heat.

Pre-emergence control: None.

Post-emergence control: A difficult to control weed; 2,4-D and mecoprop will give fair control. Apply in late spring.

Henbit. Broadleaf. Annual.

Season of fast growth: Spring and fall.

Pre-emergence control: None.

Post-emergence control: Use 2,4-D or mecoprop in fall or spring. Two applications may be required.

Comments: This weed is from the mint family, you'll notice its four-sided stem. It shows up in late winter or early spring.

Knotweed. Broadleaf. Annual.

Season of fast growth: Early spring through early fall.

Pre-emergence control: None.

Post-emergence control: Mecoprop or dicamba are the favored treatment anytime throughout season of most active growth beginning in early spring.

Comments: A common weed in hard, compacted soils. Thorough aerification may help.

Mallow, cheeseweed. Broadleaf. Annual.

Season of fast growth: Has a long growing season. Gets started in early spring and survives through fall. A difficult weed to control.

Pre-emergence control: None.

Post-emergence control: Use 2,4-D, mecoprop, or dicamba mid- to late-spring.

Mouse-ear chickweed. Broadleaf. Perennial.

Season of fast growth: Cool weather of spring or fall.

Pre-emergence control: None.

Post-emergence control: Mecoprop. Apply in fall or in early spring when temperatures are between 60° and 70° F.

Oxalis. Broadleaf. Perennial.

Season of fast growth: Spring and late summer to fall.

Pre-emergence control: None.

Post-emergence control: Products containing 2,4-D and dicamba may be used. Apply in spring or fall on a day when the wind is still and air temperatures will remain above 60°F, but below 80°F. In many areas, late summer to fall treatment is most effective. Not easy to kill; usually requires several treatments.

Plantain. Broadleaf. Perennial.

Season of fast growth: A cool-season weed. Forms rosettes with prominently veined leaves.

Pre-emergence control: None.

Post-emergence control: 2,4-D or mecoprop are very effective, applied spring or fall before formation of flower spikes.

Purslane. Broadleaf. Annual.

Season of fast growth: Summer.

Pre-emergence control: DCPA applied early to mid-spring.

Post-emergence control: Use 2,4-D mid- to late-summer.

Quackgrass. Narrowleaf. Perennial.

Season of fast growth: Spring and fall.

Pre-emergence treatment: None.

Post-emergence control: No selective control. Spot treat with dalapon or glyphosate.

Comments: Underground stems are vigorous, even digging out by hand is rarely successful.

Spotted spurge. Broadleaf. Annual.

Season of fast growth: Most aggressive growth is from late spring through early fall. A summer weed.

Pre-emergence control: Use DCPA or siduron in early spring before germination then again in mid-summer.

Post-emergence control: Products containing 2,4-D and dicamba may be used.

Comments: Minor damage may result to turfgrasses from summer treatments.

Tall fescue. Narrowleaf. Perennial.

Season of fast growth: A perennial, but grows fastest in spring and fall.

Pre-emergence control: None.

Post-emergence control: Spot treat only. Use either repeated sprays with a contact herbicide or dalapon. Glyphosate applied any time the weed is actively growing will also give good control.

Comments: Frequently confused with crabgrass. Can be dug out by hand.

Thistle. Broadleaf. Perennial.

Season of fast growth: Strongest growth occurs in cool weather of fall and spring.

Pre-emergence control: None.

Post-emergence control: 2,4-D is effective. Spray in fall. Two applications may be necessary.

Comments: There are several different types, commonly found in northern regions. Leaf forms frequently vary. Roots may spread underground horizontally.

White clover. Broadleaf. Perennial.

Season of fast growth: Cool seasons of fall and spring. Profuse flowering in early summer.

Pre-emergence control: None.

Post-emergence control: Mecoprop or dicamba in spring or fall. Choose a warm and windless day.

Wild onion, wild garlic. Broadleaf. Perennial.

Season of fast growth: Spring to mid-summer.

Pre-emergence control: None.

Post-emergence control: 2,4-D is used. May need several treatments; 2,4-D wax impregnated bars are most effective. Best used in late fall when weeds are still small. Once mature they are difficult to control.

Insects and pests

There's a patch of dead grass next to the driveway or a dead spot under the oak — was it caused by insects? The most difficult and important part of any lawn problem is diagnosing the cause.

Hundreds of kinds of insects and similar creatures live in a typical lawn. Some are so tiny they're hardly visible; or others are quite large. Most do little damage to the lawn itself, and you're not even aware of their presence. Other insects which are troublesome to people make their homes in lawns, but do not damage the grass. Fleas and ticks are in this category. But only a few serious lawn pests, such as sod webworm, the grubs of various beetles, and chinch bugs can destroy a lawn within a short time if conditions are right for their development.

The questions are: How to tell if the problem is caused by insects or a disease (or something else, such as gasoline or a dog). And if it is caused by insects, how can the damage be stopped.

Diagnosing the problem

In trying to discover the source of lawn damage, the easiest and most reliable method is to look, and look closely. Get down on your hands and knees and chances are, you will be able to see the pest in action. Some appear only at night, or only in a shady spot, or in a sunny corner. Specific habits and characteristics of the most common lawn pests are noted on the following pages.

Discovering insects in your lawn does not necessarily mean you have to spray. If there is a problem try to link in some definite way the symptom to the pest. For example, look for the green pellet-like droppings left by sod webworm. Remember too that damage is hardly visible until the pest population has built up to a considerable extent.

Many insects are only troublesome to certain kinds of grass. For instance, chinch bugs are by far most damaging to St. Augustinegrass. Wireworms rarely attack any grasses besides bahia or centipede. There are many examples like these. So to the extent possible, choose a grass that's not bothered or at least doesn't have a number one enemy.

Grow a healthy lawn. We don't intend to make that sound simple or the solution to all problems, but a well-maintained lawn will be much less subject to serious insect damage.

It is also able to recover quickly if problems do occur.

Finally, if your lawn is a perfect, frequently watered and fertilized putter's delight, be prepared for some extra pest-related chores. In such a prime environment, more insect eggs are laid and more will survive.

Controlling lawn pests with chemicals

Insecticides are not the only answer to lawn pest problems. But, if and when you decide they are necessary, we feel you should know about them. There are many forms of insecticides available. If used properly, they are relatively harmless.

Here are some brief descriptions of insecticides commonly used by homeowners to control lawn pests. For the sake of simplification, we have listed the most frequently used trade or chemical name.

Aspon: This is a good control for chinch bugs and sod webworm. It works fast and is effective up to two months. Water the lawn before spraying, then withhold water for two or three days to permit the chemical to do its job. Keep off the lawn until the chemical has been washed into the soil.

Baygon: Similar to Sevin (see below). Frequently used in baits. Controls chinch bugs, earwigs, leafhoppers.

Carbaryl: Also known as Sevin. This chemical has been around a long time and is available in a wide variety of forms from many manufacturers. It has several uses for home lawn insect control.

Diazinon: Like carbaryl, widely available in many forms. One of the best for grub control. Protects against several lawn pests up to four to six weeks.

Chlorpyrifos: This is more commonly known by its trade name, Dursban. It provides effective control on chinch bugs, grubs, and sod webworm and many other insect pests as well. It remains effective for four to six weeks.

Metaldehyde: Look for this ingredient in slug and snail baits. Use it where snails hide, such as around ground covers. Both snails and slugs hide in cool, moist areas during the day and come out at night. They love new lawns and dichondra.

Methoxyclor: A common ingredient in many spray mixes. Generally, it is very useful and has about a two-month residual.

Mesurol: This is a very effective killer of slugs and snails. Lightly water the area before spreading the bait.

Milky disease: (Biological control) This is a disease natural to Japanese beetle grubs. It has no effect on other kinds of grubs or any other insects. It is established in soils over a period of years where Japanese beetles are present. It is slow to establish and control is not one hundred percent, but it will keep the beetles in check.

Bacillus thuringensis: (Biological control) Similar to milky spore disease in that it is very specific. It will kill only caterpillars (butterfly and moth larvae). Very useful in many situations, although it is not widely used on lawns.

Of course, the best information on these and other pest control products is on the product label. We must stress, read the label in the nursery or garden shop before purchase and again, carefully, before use.

Identifying pest damage

Lawn damaging insects can be conveniently grouped according to where they are most active, above or below the ground, and the type of damage they do. Control methods are different for each group.

Live above the soil surface and suck plant juices — chinch bugs, leafhoppers, spider mites, and similar pests.

To control:
✓ Mow the lawn.
✓ Remove clippings.
✓ Water heavily.
✓ Wait until grass blades are dry, then apply insecticide according to label directions. Do not water for two days.

Live at the soil surface and feed on leaves — sod webworms, cutworms, armyworms, and fiery skipper larvae.

To control:
✓ Mow the lawn.
✓ Remove clippings.
✓ Water heavily.
✓ Wait until grass blades are dry, then apply insecticide according to label directions. Best applied in late afternoon when insects are active.
✓ Do not water for two days.
✓ Fertilize to aid in recovery of the lawn, if the season is appropriate.

Live below the soil surface and feed on roots — grubs, wireworms, ground pearls.

To control:
✓ Mow the lawn.
✓ Remove clippings.
✓ Apply recommended insecticide according to label directions. Water heavily immediately after spraying, but not so much that the insecticide washes away.
✓ Fertilize to aid in recovery of the lawn if the season is appropriate.

Sod webworm

Symptom: In late spring look for small dead patches 1 to 2 inches in diameter among the normal growing grass. By midsummer. these may be large dead patches. The most severe damage usually occurs in July and August. Sod webworms chew grass blades off just above the thatch line and pull the blades into a silken tunnel to eat them. Eventually, the small patches will coalesce, forming large, irregular dead patches.

Description: The adult form of the webworm is a buff colored moth with a wing span of about one inch. They fly in a jerky, zig-zag pattern, just a few feet above the lawn. The moths don't damage the lawn but they drop eggs into the grass that, upon hatching develop into very hungry caterpillars.

Sod webworms feed at night. Look for them by carefully breaking apart the damaged areas with your fingers. Other evidence is their green-tan excrement, little pellets about the size of a pin head. Also, flocks of birds feeding on the lawn may indicate large populations of sod webworm. When sod webworms are suspected, they can be forced to the surface of the grass by drenching 1 square foot area with 1 gallon of soapy water.
(Use ¼ cup of laundry or household detergent per gallon.)

Control: Aspon, diazinon, Dursban, Sevin, Baygon.

Grubs

Symptoms: Distinct brown patches, usually irregular in shape. Since the grubs eat grass roots, the dead grass pulls loose easily. If the dead patch of grass rolls back easily like a section of carpet, you can be pretty sure it is caused by below-ground grubs. They are most damaging in late spring or early fall. If you see more than two C-shaped grubs in a square foot area, the patch should be treated. As with sod webworm, another sign of grubs is unusual numbers of birds or moles around the lawn. They know the grubs are there and are looking to make a dinner of them.

Checking for grubs.

June beetle   May beetle   Masked chafer   *Ataenus spretulus*   European chafer (top) *Phyllophaga crinita*

Actual size

Description: Grubs are the larvae of many kinds of beetles. They are whitish or grayish in color with brown heads and dark hind parts. The adult beetles appear in late spring or summer and feed on shade trees or garden shrubs.

Control: If your lawn is already infested with grubs, keep in mind they are insulated by a layer of grass leaves and soil. The insecticide must get to this depth in the soil by repeated heavy waterings. Use products that contain diazinon or Dursban.

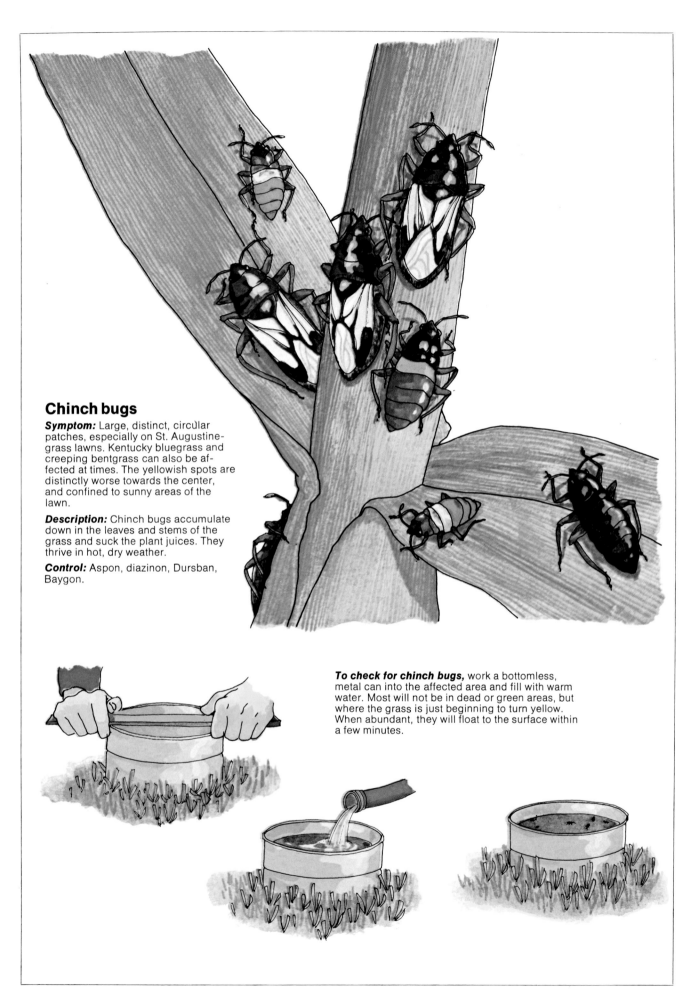

Chinch bugs

Symptom: Large, distinct, circular patches, especially on St. Augustine-grass lawns. Kentucky bluegrass and creeping bentgrass can also be affected at times. The yellowish spots are distinctly worse towards the center, and confined to sunny areas of the lawn.

Description: Chinch bugs accumulate down in the leaves and stems of the grass and suck the plant juices. They thrive in hot, dry weather.

Control: Aspon, diazinon, Dursban, Baygon.

To check for chinch bugs, work a bottomless, metal can into the affected area and fill with warm water. Most will not be in dead or green areas, but where the grass is just beginning to turn yellow. When abundant, they will float to the surface within a few minutes.

Billbug

Symptom: A small and distinct circular pattern becomes yellowish or brown. Adult billbugs feed on stems, while grubs of billbugs feed on roots. Most damage is caused in late summer. Grass stems within the dead areas lift easily out of the soil.

Description: Different species of billbugs prefer different types of grass. In the southern-most regions, bermuda and zoysiagrass are commonly attacked, while in the northern regions, Kentucky bluegrass is preferred.

Control. Use an insecticide such as diazinon or Baygon in mid-summer if you find more than one billbug grub per square foot.

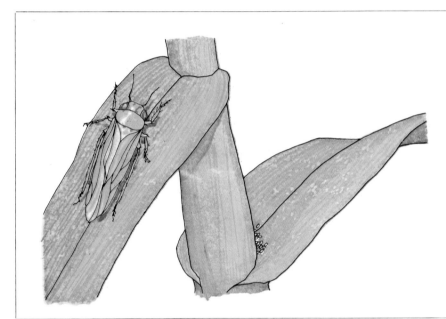

Leafhopper

Symptom: These tiny insects are nearly always present to some degree on the surface of lawns. When severe, they can wipe out a newly seeded lawn and cause a mature lawn to look bleached and unhealthy.

Description: They are tiny, even when full grown. Their color is usually green, but may be yellow or grey. If your lawn has a lot of them, each step through the grass will kick a swarm.

Control: Insecticide treatments are usually not necessary, they may be more of a nuisance to you than the lawn. Diazinon will effectively control them if necessary.

Mole cricket

Symptom: Irregular streaks of brown and wilted grass. Most common on bahiagrass, bermuda, St. Augustine and sometimes centipede and zoysiagrass. The dead grass will pull up easily. You can find the tunnels with your fingers.

Description: Mole crickets are about 1½ to 2 inches long and brown or greyish brown. They look similar to a common cricket, except their head is large and notable. Their front legs, which they use for digging, are especially large. They feed on the turf roots and, by tunneling, cause nearby roots to dry out.

Control: Baits for mole cricket containing Baygon are most common. Apply the bait the evening before a warm night and water the lawn first. Or use diazinon, in spring, about a week after seeing the first signs of mole cricket activity.

Armyworms, cutworms, and fiery skipper

Symptoms: These three moth larvae chew off the grass blades above the soil surface. The damage they cause is very similar to sod webworm. Armyworms cause round, bare areas in lawns. If there are many of them, the grass will be eaten to the soil level. Cutworms also feed on the grass leaves, cutting them off near the surface. Fiery skippers are usually a minor problem, but can be serious pests of bentgrass and bermudagrass lawns, especially hybrid bermuda. They can also be a problem on bluegrass lawns in some areas.

Descriptions: Skippers are easy to distinguish from other pests. They're about an inch long and brownish yellow, with very distinct dark brown heads and thin necks. Cutworms are plump, smooth, and almost always curled when you find them. They're usually brown to nearly black, but some are spotted and some are striped. Armyworms are yellowish white and have an upsidedown "Y" on their head.

Control: Products that contain diazinon, Dursban, or Sevin are all useful.

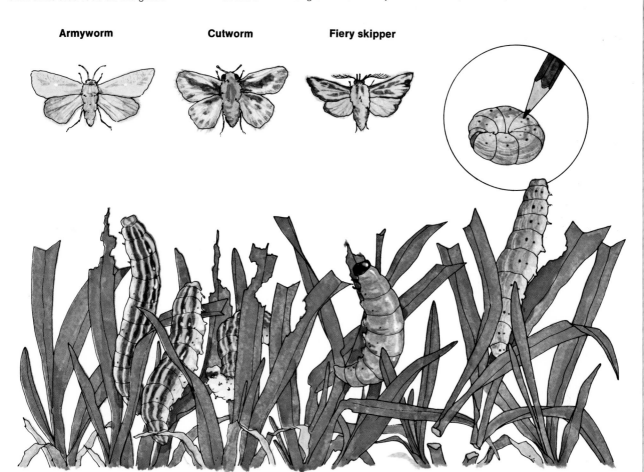

| Armyworm | Cutworm | Fiery skipper |

Nuisance pests

Brown dog tick
This pest is most common to lawns that are near wooded areas. Ticks will be most active in spring and early summer. *DON'T* try to get them off with a hot match. Diazinon, Dursban or Sevin are good lawn sprays.

Ants
Ants are a problem in lawns because of the nest mounds they make, not because they feed directly on, or otherwise harm the grass. Diazinon granules, Dursban, or diazinon sprays will control them for up to two months.

Gnats
A type of tiny fly, they're similar to mosquitos in many ways; most need water to lay eggs. They can be annoying when they swarm around the lawn. The best treatment is a fogging spray.

Earwigs
These hard, dark reddish brown insects hide in dark places during the day. Their pincers aren't nearly as dangerous as they look; they're only useful against other earwigs. Baits containing Baygon, scattered in the evening, are very effective, or spray with diazinon, Dursban, or Sevin.

Chiggers
Chiggers are not insects. They are actually tiny spiders or mites. Their eggs are laid in the soil. After hatching, the larvae crawl up onto the grass or weeds waiting for an animal to brush by. Repellents containing diethyltoluamide are effective as well as sprays of diazinon.

Fleas
These are certainly well-known pests to dog or cat owners. They may fall off a pet and wait in the lawn for another host animal. The insecticides diazinon, malathion, and Sevin are good controls.

Occasional lawn pests

Some of the insects and other pests included in this group can, in specific situations, cause extensive damage. But they are not nearly so common as sod webworm, grubs, and chinch bugs. Several are problems only in relatively confined regions. Others, such as wireworms, sowbugs, pillbugs, millipedes, and centipedes are widespread but rarely cause serious damage.

Ground pearl
These tiny "pearls" are attached to the roots of bermudagrass and centipedegrass. About an ⅛ inch in diameter, they damage the grass by feeding on the roots. No chemical control is presently used.

Sowbugs and pillbugs
These are very similar looking but pillbugs are the ones that can roll themselves into a ball. Usually they make dinner only on decaying organic matter. Control with diazinon.

Spittlebugs
They rarely cause much damage on lawns but are a common inhabitant. They *do* damage other plants. While feeding, they hide themselves under a material that looks just like spittle, hence the name. If necessary, they can be controlled by either Sevin or diazinon.

Wireworm
These larva of click-beetle feed on lawn roots. They're about an inch long and brown. Only when populations build up will they damage lawns. Look for them in the root zone of the sections of dead grass. Diazinon may be used for control.

Periodical cicada
These are large insects that live deep in the soil for several years. When they leave the ground, a large number of holes are made. The adults damage nearby shrubs and trees rather than the lawn.

Millipedes and centipedes
Rarely damaging to lawns, they are often found in or near them. Like sowbugs, they like cool, moist hiding spots. If there are too many in your yard, a good clean-up of trash or wood will eliminate them.

Grasshoppers
These will damage your lawn only if a great many move in at one time. They are usually most abundant in late summer and in more rural or suburban areas. Control with Dursban.

Crickets
These won't eat much of your lawn but may be a problem especially as they try to move into your house for winter. Use diazinon granules or similar chemical control around the house if they become a problem.

Lawn diseases and similar problems

As we mentioned in the section, "Insects and pests," diagnosing lawn problems can often be difficult, especially if considerable time has elapsed between the cause of the damage and the diagnosis. Many times the problem will be attributed to an insect or disease, when actually the climate, environmental conditions, or cultural practices are the cause. Mowing height, competition from tree roots, chlorosis, soil compaction, improper watering, and herbicide damage are some of the many factors that either cause the symptoms or are related to the development of the disease.

The importance of proper lawn care

It is repeated again and again in this book that proper maintenance will reduce lawn problems. This is especially true when it comes to lawn disease. Most of the diseases that attack typical home lawns are due to improper management. Thatch is one of the most important factors that govern the frequency of disease in the home lawn. Thatch restricts the movement of air, water, and fertilizers into the soil, and generally weakens the lawn. This type of lawn is naturally much more disease prone.

When and how much you fertilize also has an important impact on dis-

ease development. An over-fertilized lawn, as well as an under-fertilized lawn, are more disease susceptible. Timing is also critical. For example, if you give a cool-season lawn heavy doses of growth-stimulating fertilizer in late spring and summer (periods of naturally slow growth), it becomes increasingly susceptible to leaf spot and *Fusarium* blight. It's important to follow a fertilizer program that conforms to the growth cycle of your particular lawn grass. The lawn experts say it best: "Let the grass grow, don't make it grow."

Watering practices also relate to disease frequency. Lawns that are watered deeply but infrequently usually have fewer disease problems. Constantly wet grass in poorly drained soil promotes disease.

Lawn diseases are easier to prevent than to cure. Follow these steps to prevent diseases from becoming established in your lawn.

✓ Plant a grass type and variety that is adapted to your climate.

✓ Mow at the proper height.

✓ Fertilize at recommended rates and on a schedule that fits the growth cycle of your cool- or warm-season grass.

✓ Water deeply and infrequently and only when the lawn needs it.

When a serious disease does attack your lawn despite adherence to these preventive measures, use of a chemical control is necessary.

Fungicides

There are over a dozen chemicals commonly sprayed on lawns by homeowners to prevent and control disease. They are categorized as either "systemic" or "non-systemic."

Systemic fungicides work from inside the plant, so are usually the most effective. They are, however, very specific and will control only certain diseases.

Non-systemic fungicides work from outside the plant. They are best used before a disease starts. For example, if you know from past experience a certain disease will attack your lawn in two weeks or so, start spraying the appropriate fungicide now. This way the disease can be prevented.

Look at the chart for a breakdown on the uses of the various fungicides. Use the succeeding pages to help identify and control any diseases that occur in your lawn. For the sake of simplification, chemical names rather than trade names are used to describe controls in the disease descriptions.

Common fungicides

Common Name/ Trade Name	Uses
anilazine/ Dyrene	Dollar spot and melting out, rust, snow mold. Non-systemic.
benomyl/ Benlate Tersan 1991 Cleary 3336	Brown patch, dollar spot, *Fusarium* patch, *Fusarium* blight, powdery mildew, and stripe smut. Has systemic action.
captan/ Orthocide	Melting out, damping off, and stripe smut. Non-systemic, contact only.
chlorothalonil/ Daconil 2787 Bravo	Brown patch, dollar spot, *Fusarium* patch, melting out, and red thread. Non-systemic fungicide.
chloroneb/ Tersan SP Demosan	*Pythium* blight, grey snow mold. Non-systemic.
cycloheximide/ Acti-dione	Brown patch, dollar spot, leaf spot, melting out, powdery mildew, snow mold. Non-systemic.
diazoben/ Dexon	Damping off, *pythium* (grease spot). Non-systemic.
ethazol Koban Truban	*Pythium*. Non-systemic.
folpet/ Phaltan	Melting out. Non-systemic, contact only.
mancozeb/ Dithane M-45 Fore	Red thread, rust, and melting out. Non-systemic.
maneb/ Dithane M-22	Rust. Non-systemic.
oxycarboxin/ Plantvax	Rust. Non-systemic.
PCNB/ Terraclor	Brown patch. Melting out. Slight systemic activity.
thiabendazole/ Mertect 140F.	Brown patch, dollar spot, *Fusarium* patch, snow mold. Non-systemic.
thiophanate methyl/Topsin Spot Clean Fungo-50	Brown patch, dollar spot, *Fusarium* blight, *Fusarium* patch, stripe smut. Systemic.
thiram/ Tersan 75	Should be combined with other fungicide.

Disease trouble shooting

Looking closely:	Cause
Fungus growth can be seen on the blade:	
Black, long streaks of powdery spores	Stripe smut
White and powdery	Powdery mildew
Red or orange, like a powder	Rust
Grey and easily rubbed off	Slime mold
Visible spots on leaves, actual fungus is not visible (just the results of fungus infection):	
Reddish brown to blue-black and circular or oval	Leaf spot (melting out)
Straw colored bands with a reddish brown border	Dollar spot
Looking at the whole lawn	**Cause**
The diseased area is circular:	
Present in late winter or early spring	Snow mold
Present in spring, summer, or fall	
One inch to four feet or more in diameter	
Mushrooms just inside or outside the circle	Fairy ring
No mushrooms	Brown patch
One to eight inches in diameter	
Small, with many throughout the lawn	Dollar spot
Only in full sun and with green centers (frog-eye)	*Fusarium* blight
In low areas and often in streaks	Pythium
The diseased area is irregular in shape:	
New lawn seedlings wilt and die	Damping-off
Mature lawn affected, spots on leaves	Melting-out (leaf spot)
Mature lawn affected, thin, no spots on leaves	Nematodes

Note: Due to space limitations, not all lawn diseases will be in this chart; this is only a helpful guide.

Common lawn diseases

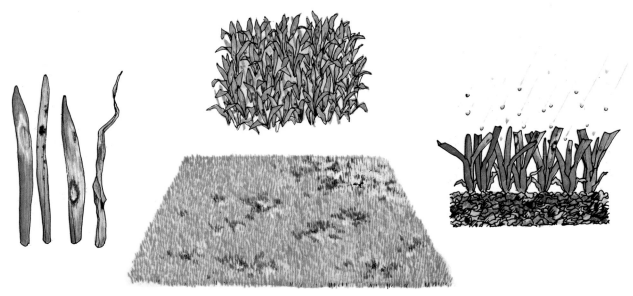

Melting out, leaf spot:
April to November

Description: Melting out refers to a number of leaf spot diseases favoring Kentucky bluegrass, fescue, and bermudagrass. The most obvious symptom of the disease is elongated circular spots on the leaves. These spots have a brown or straw-colored center with black to purplish borders.

Favorable climatic conditions: Cool, (50° to 70°F.) moist conditions are most favorable; first appears in the shade. Most severe in closely mowed lawns.

Susceptible grasses: 'Park' and 'Delta' Kentucky bluegrass are very susceptible.

Resistant varieties: 'Merion' and 'Adelphi' Kentucky bluegrass. Many of the newer improved bluegrass varieties also have good resistance.

Cultural control: Reduce shade. Improve aeration and water drainage. Mow at recommended height.

Chemical control: Anilazine, captan, chlorothalonil, cycloheximide, folpet, and mancozeb.

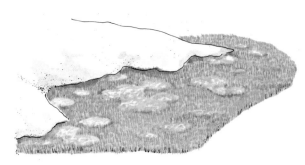

Fusarium patch:
September to May

Description: This disease is called pink snow mold if it develops under snow or at the margins of a melting snow bank. It causes circular patches 1 to 8 inches in diameter. Tiny white or pink masses are sometimes seen on dead leaves. Fungal threads, also white or pink, can be seen in early morning.

Favorable climatic conditions: Cool (40° to 60°F.) temperatures and moisture.

Susceptible grasses: Ryegrass, fescue, zoysiagrass, and colonial and creeping bentgrass.

Resistant grasses: Improved Kentucky bluegrass.

Cultural control: Reduce shade, if any. Improve soil aeration and drainage. Avoid excess nitrogen fertilization in the fall.

Chemical control: Benomyl, chlorothalonil, mancozeb, thiabendazole.

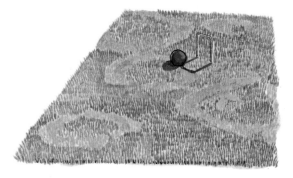

Fusarium blight:
May to October

Description: The disease begins as scattered light green patches ½ to 8 inches in diameter, that turn dull tan to reddish-brown. The most diagnostic of these larger diseased paches in the lawn is the "frog-eye" pattern. This is an apparently healthy green patch of grass partially or completely surrounded by a ring of dead grass.

Favorable climatic conditions: Hot, dry, and windy weather is especially favorable. It occurs most commonly in areas that have suffered water stress.

Susceptible grasses: Of the Kentucky bluegrasses, 'Arboretum,' 'Fylking,' 'Park,' and 'Dennstar.'

Resistant varieties: 'Glade,' 'Parade,' 'Sydsport,' 'Columbia,' 'Adelphi,' and Kentucky bluegrass.

Cultural control: Avoid heavy fertilization and follow correct watering and mowing practices. Light frequent watering will help during drought.

Chemical control: Benomyl and thiophanate have been most useful but control is difficult. Water the night before and thoroughly drench fungicide into turf.

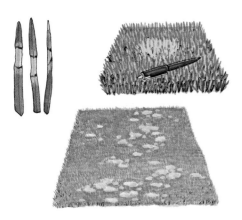

Dollar spot:
May to November

Description: A common fungus disease that attacks several different types of grass, but is most severe on bermuda and bentgrass. It kills in small spots from 3 inches to 12 inches in diameter, but the spots may coalesce into large areas. Diseased spots are usually bleached from tan to straw-colored.

Favorable climatic conditions: Moderate temperatures, excess moisture, and heavy thatch all contribute to this disease. Underfertilized lawns are more prone.

Susceptible grasses: Bentgrass, Kentucky bluegrass, bermudagrass, ryegrass, and fescues.

Resistant varieties: Some of the new, improved Kentucky bluegrasses.

Cultural control: Increase nitrogen, keep thatch at a minimum, water deeply when necessary.

Chemical control: Anilazine, benomyl, chlorothalonil, thiabendazole.

Brown patch:
July to August

Description: Recognize it by the large irregular, circular areas, which can be up to several feet in diameter. The patches usually have a brownish to grey discoloration, with a water-soaked appearance around the edges of the patch. Normally, only the leaves and stems are attacked.

Favorable climatic conditions: High temperatures (75° to 95°F), excessive thatch, high humidity, lush growth from over-fertilization, and excessive moisture are perfect for this disease.

Susceptible grasses: A serious disease in the South on centipede and St. Augustinegrass. It also attacks bentgrass, bermudagrass, dichondra, ryegrass, fescue and zoysiagrass.

Resistant grasses: Improved Kentucky bluegrass.

Cultural control: Avoid heavy nitrogen fertilization, reduce shading, and water deeply when necessary.

Chemical control: Benomyl, thiophonate, chlorothalonil.

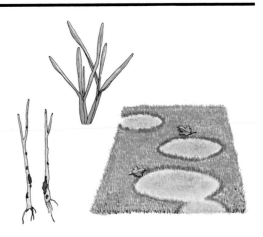

Pythium, grease spot or cottony blight:
July and August

Description: Generally a problem on newly established lawns but will occur on any lawn if conditions are favorable. The diseased area may be a few inches to several feet in diameter. It frequently occurs in small, circular spots about 2 inches across on closely cut lawns. Look for it in early morning while dew is still on the grass, or during humid weather. The diseased areas are surrounded by blackened blades covered with a white or grey fungus. Dry weather will stop the disease.

Favorable climatic conditions: High temperatures and excess moisture.

Susceptible grasses: Ryegrass, tall fescue, bentgrass, bermudagrass, and bluegrass.

Resistant varieties: None.

Cultural control: Avoid excessive watering during warm weather, don't overfertilize. Seed late in the fall.

Chemical control: Use a fungicide such a diazoben, mancozeb, koban or thiram at first sign of the disease.

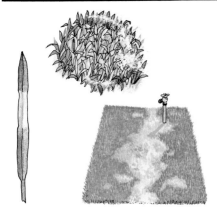

Damping off:
Seedling lawns

Description: New seedings fail to fill in properly. If possible, look closely and you can see young seedlings have emerged from the soil, but collapsed. This disease is caused by a number of different fungal organisms.

Favorable climatic conditions: Overwatering after seeding especially if soil is heavy and days are overcast. No problem if starting from sprigs or stolons.

Susceptible grasses. Any seeded grass.

Resistant varieties: None.

Cultural control: Make sure pH is nearly neutral. Do not overwater and provide good drainage.

Chemical control: Use seeds treated with captan or thiram or spray captan or thiram at first sign of trouble.

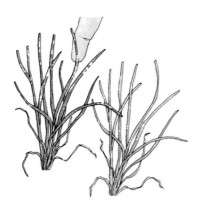

Powdery mildew:
July to November

Description: First symptoms are light patches of dusty, white to light grey growth on grass blades. Lowest leaves may become completely covered. Generally not too serious a problem, but can be severe. Most common in shady areas.

Favorable climatic conditions: Slow or non-existant air circulation and shade are the most common causes.

Susceptible grasses: Kentucky bluegrass (especially 'Merion'), zoysia and bermudagrass.

Resistant varieties: 'Glade,' 'Nugget,' and 'Birka' Kentucky bluegrass; 'Fortress,' red fescue.

Cultural control: Reduce shade, if possible. Don't overwater. Avoid overfertilization.

Chemical control: Benomyl, cycloheximide.

Rust:
July to November

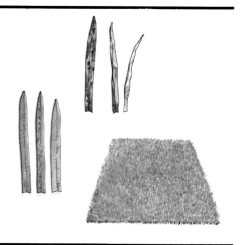

Description: This disease is appropriately named. The affected lawn will have a rust-colored cast noticeable from a distance. Close-up, the dustlike rust spores are in circular or long groups on grass leaves. The rust rarely causes severe damage to home lawns but are very serious where grasses are grown for seed.

Favorable climatic conditions: Moderately warm, moist weather. Dew that lasts on the lawn for 10 to 12 hours is enough to promote germination of the fungus spores. Any stress conditions which restrict growth of the lawn grass favors the development of rust.

Susceptible grasses: Most all commonly grown grasses can be affected by rust. Kentucky bluegrass and the ryegrasses are most frequently damaged.

Resistant grasses: Fine fescues.

Cultural control: Keep the lawn growing rapidly by fertilizing with nitrogen and frequent watering. Then, mow frequently, every four or five days.

Chemical control: Maneb, anilazine, and oxycarboxin are moderately effective.

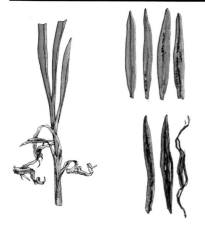

Stripe smut:
April to November

Description: Diseased plants are usually pale green and stunted. Long black stripes of spores are visible on the leaf blades. Affected leaves curl, die, and become shredded by the advancing disease.

Favorable climatic conditions: Moderate temperatures of spring and fall. Hot and dry weather will often halt the disease.

Susceptible grasses: Kentucky bluegrass and bentgrass are commonly attacked.

Resistant grasses: 'A-34,' 'Adelphi,' and 'Sydsport' are some of the many Kentucky bluegrasses that are resistant.

Cultural control: Keep thatch to a minimum and avoid overwatering.

Chemical control: Two systemics, benomyl and thiophanate will provide some control. Best applied in late fall.

Typhula blight, grey snow mold:
Any time with snow

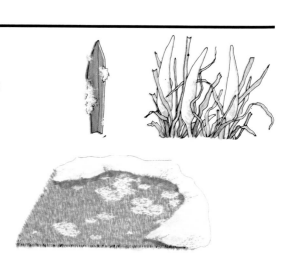

Description: First appears as vaguely straw or tan-colored circular areas, a few inches to a few feet in diameter. The dead grass may actually be covered at some point with a greyish fungal growth. It occurs primarily in the northern United States and Canada, not reaching as far south as pink snow mold.

Favorable climatic conditions: A deep snow cover that is slow to melt.

Suspectible grasses: Most all the cool-season grasses.

Resistant grasses: None.

Cultural control: Be sure the lawn is not succulent or lush (overfertilized with nitrogen) before the first snowfall. Also, avoid excessive use of lime. Keep thatch layer to a minimum.

Chemical control: Apply anilazine or thiram in the fall before the first snowfall is forecast. Snow mold (pink and gray) is often only found in areas where snow lies for a long time, such as against a house or garage. These areas may be all that will need treatment.

Grey leaf spot of St. Augustinegrass:
June through August

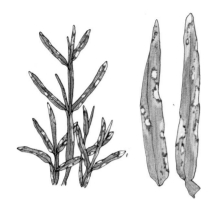

Description: Commonly attacks St. Augustinegrass, especially recently sprigged or plugged lawns. Mostly on the leaves but some symptoms on the stems too. The spots on the leaves are round and ash-to-brown in color. They are surrounded by a dark margin. The most serious effect of the disease is this scorching or dying back of the leaves. Seldom will it kill an entire lawn.

Favorable climatic conditions: Warm rainy periods of summer.

Susceptible grasses: St. Augustinegrass.

Resistant varieties: 'Roselawn' has shown some resistance.

Cultural control: Do not overfertilize with nitrogen and water as infrequently as the lawn will tolerate. When you do water, however, be sure the moisture penetrates to at least five inches. Prune shade trees if possible, to increase light and air circulation.

Chemical control: Chlorothalonil, anilazine, mancozeb, maneb, captan.

St. Augustinegrass Decline (SAD):
Anytime

Description: This is a virus disease that causes a mottling of the leaf blade, overall yellowing, and a general decline in the lawns vigor. A St. Augustine-grass lawn attacked by SAD will generally be invaded by bermudagrass and weeds which are not affected.

Favorable climatic conditions: Known to occur only in Texas and Louisiana.

Susceptible grasses: Only St. Augustinegrass.

Resistant varieties. At present, 'Floratam' St. Augustinegrass.

Cultural control: If your lawn is infected, the only control is to plant plugs of 'Floratam' into the middle of the infested areas. It will eventually replace the diseased grass.

Chemical control: None.

Fairy ring:
April to November

Description: Appears as a ring of dark green grass surrounding areas of dead or light-colored grass. The rings can be produced by the growth of any one of over 50 different kinds of fungus. The dying grass in the ring is caused by lack of water penetration.

Favorable climatic conditions: Fairy rings will develop in soils that contain undecomposed woody organic matter, such as dead tree roots or old construction materials. Primarily a problem in acid soils.

Susceptible grasses: All.

Resistant grasses. None.

Cultural control: Try to keep the lawn growing by applying adequate nitrogen fertilizer to hide the problem. Aerate the ring to improve water penetration. Keep areas wet for about two weeks, and mow frequently.

Chemical control: It's best to try to live with it. Complete eradication with a soil fumigant is difficult.

Nematodes

Description: Nematodes are very common in the soil. These small worms are so small you need a microscope to see them, but scientists say they are the most common form of life on earth. There are thousands of different kinds, but only a few damage plants.

Symptoms: The grass will be generally unthrifty, thin, yellowish and drought susceptible in summer. It will not respond to other treatments such as aeration, fertilization, or watering. Upon inspection of the roots, they will be stubby, shallow, and possibly show swellings or galls. Complete diagnosis requires a microscope.

Control: Keep the grass as healthy as possible. If the presence of damaging nematodes is confirmed by a professional, consult with an experienced pest control operator or your County Extension Agent.

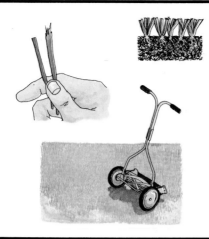

Scalping and dull mower injury

Lawn scalping occurs whenever too much of the grass plant is cut off at one time. Reducing the height of the lawn by more than one-third creates a severe shock, but the results may not be immediately visible. When the mower blades dip down, suddenly removing most of the green part and the leaf blade of the lawn, the effects are obvious and should not be confused with insect or disease damage.

If your mower blades are dull, the lawn will have a greyish cast a day or so after mowing. This happens when the leaf tips have been shredded instead of cut, thus turning brown. This is especially noticeable when the weather is dry. Besides being unsightly, shredded tips are an easy entry point for many disease organisms.

Chemical burn

Many lawns are damaged by spilled fertilizer, herbicide, gasoline, or by dog urination. These types of injuries are characterized by distinct and abrupt patches of dead grass. The damage of dog urination is slightly more confusing. It is characterized by bright green grass surrounding a patch of dead grass. The solution to these problems is to thoroughly drench the soil with water. If this doesn't work, you'll have to replace the soil under the dead spot and repatch the damaged area. (See page 56 for patching instructions.)

Summer drying out

Drying out affects all grasses and can do considerable damage. It's easy to see but often mistaken for insect or disease damage. The soil could be compacted in one area or the sprinklers just missed a spot.

The first indication of insufficient water is when part of the lawn changes color from bright green to dull green. Then, if your footprints don't spring back in a reasonable length of time, water stress is confirmed.

If you have a cool-season grass, raise the cutting height at least one-half inch and water deeply. Check the soil moisture occasionally with a soil probe or moisture meter. If one area begins to show signs of drought, use a portable sprinkler or a hand held hose to soak the area. See the section on watering, pages 34 to 39.

Nitrogen or iron deficiency

Nitrogen is the nutrient needed by lawns in the greatest quantity. The actual amount will vary with the type of grass, but most need some lawn fertilizer every year. If you haven't been applying fertilizer, your lawn will probably be slightly yellow and not growing as well as it could.

If you have fertilized adequately and the lawn is still yellow and slow growing, the problem could be a lack of iron or improper pH. Some grasses, centipedegrass for instance, are especially sensitive to a lack of iron. A typical lawn fertilizer applied on a lawn that needs iron may actually increase the yellowish look. Apply iron either as a liquid spray or as a supplemental, granular, dry lawn application which is available in combination with nitrogen and sulfur.

Growing lawns in the shade

The establishment and care of a good quality lawn in the shade is a real headache for many people. It need not be. Many beautiful lawns are grown in the shade of spreading trees. One of the measures of success is understanding the relationship between the tree and the grass underneath.

First of all, you must realize that there are many types of shade — light, half, dappled, full, and heavy. Few grasses will grow in full or heavy shade. Although it's difficult to figure out exactly, a lawn needs about 50 percent of the sunlight passing through a tree to sustain it underneath.

Beating the competition

The grass growing underneath your trees is competing with the trees for water and nutrients, but most importantly, light. If left alone, and the shade is heavy enough, the tree will almost always win. The grass will become thin and spotty or gradually die out altogether.

Your job is to supply the requirements of the grass without harming the tree. Of course, if the tree is not a functional part of the landscape, you may decide to remove it in favor of the grass.

One of the first steps towards a successful lawn in the shade is to plant a shade-tolerant grass. Grasses are listed according to their ability to grow in shade on page 19. Even within species, certain varieties are more shade tolerant than others. The variety charts on pages 16 to 18 includes such strengths.

In areas of established turf, you may want to do small scale renovation and reseed with a better adapted grass. We also know of people who reseed every year with turf-type ryegrass to keep fresh new grass under trees.

The choice of grass may require some forethought. If you have recently planted a young tree, shade probably isn't a problem now, but may be in the future.

If you are considering planting trees in your lawn, plan ahead. Choose trees which cast filtered shade, and don't overplant. Several lawn trees are listed in the section, ''Lawn tips,'' but if you really want to make an edu-cated selection, see the Ortho book *The World of Trees.*

If a suitable grass is already growing under your trees, good maintenance practices will, of course, help the shaded lawn. However, there are some slight modifications of normal practices that will help even more.

Mow the lawn higher, at the highest cut suggested on page 51. More blade length means more light trapping ability. If fertilization is desired, consider soil injections for the tree instead of applying fertilizer directly on the lawn. A major problem of grass in the shade is overfertilization.

Watering deeply (but not overwatering) is especially important when trees are growing in the lawn. Shallow watering causes surface rooting which in turn causes mowing problems and allows the tree roots to rob the lawn of its nutrient needs.

If surface roots are already a problem, most trees can stand some root pruning without doing them much harm.

Don't leave the leaves

Grasses growing in shade are more tender than those growing in full sun, so pay close attention to insect and disease problems.

Fallen leaves and heavy grass clippings can smother growing grass and increase damage from pests. This is particularly true in shaded areas.

Too much shade

The most obvious, and sometimes the simplest solution to shade, is to prune the tree. Through proper thinning, as much as 40 percent of a tree's leaf surface can be removed without drastically changing the appearance of the tree. In fact, it usually enhances it.

Sometimes there are too many trees. Removal of a few can be helpful not only for the lawn, but for the trees that remain. Also, the Ortho book, *All About Ground Covers* lists many ground covers that do well in low light. You might also want to check into other alternatives such as an attractive stone or bark mulch.

Don't give up on growing grass in the shade. Proper maintenance practices and adapted varieties make shade lawns possible in many situations. See text for more information.

Lawns in your area

These pages are really about climate, and the effects of climate on lawn growing. The length of growing season determines how much fertilizer your lawn will need each year. Summer rainfall patterns tell which lawns need irrigation systems or at least regular watering.

Obviously, winter low and summer high temperatures delineate to a great extent which grasses can be grown where.

In our earliest research, we questioned lawn owners around the country, who revealed a strong desire for specific information concerning the lawns in their climates. We heard comments like this one from Ohio: "Most lawn books are limited by various geographical problems. I would like a book on growing lawns where I live." An individual from Texas said, "None of the books about lawns have much use around here."

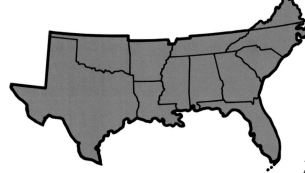

The South is big and the grass climate in Tennessee is very different from the Florida climate. Compare the climate of Miami, Florida, to that of Jackson, Tennessee, for instance. The Miami climate is almost tropical. Winter temperatures never drop anywhere near freezing and they receive an average of 60 inches of rain per year. Warm-season grasses are the rule and since the growing season is year-round, the fertilizer program goes through the whole year also.

Jackson, on the other hand, has January low temperatures that

average 15°F. This is much too low for most warm-season grasses. Although many of the zoysia and hybrid bermudagrasses make their way into Tennessee, most of the beautiful lawns in Jackson are made up of cool-season grasses — Kentucky bluegrass or fescues. This is the case with many northern or high elevation areas of the South.

Local characteristics such as soil types and summer highs or winter lows, play an important role in which type of grass you grow and how you care for it. Knowing this kind of specific information will help you grow a better lawn.

Extension information

The recommended grasses that are listed in the following were compiled from extension bulletins from each state. They are the result of years of research and experience and are one

VIRGINIA

Soil and climate. Much of Virginia is located in a transition zone where some kinds of both cool-season and warm-season grasses grow but where neither type is especially well adapted.
Lime. Normally needed if soil has not previously been limed. Apply lime as indicated by soil test results. One application lasts for at least three years and frequently much longer.
Soil testing. Check with your local County or City Extension Service Office or write:
Soil Testing Laboratory
Cooperative Extension Service
Virginia Polytechnic Institute and

State University
Blacksbury, Virginia 24061
Recommended grasses. West of the Blue Ridge Mountains and in the northern Piedmont area, the cool-season grasses should be planted. These include Kentucky bluegrass, tall fescue, the fine fescues, and turf-type perennial ryegrass.

Warm-season grasses, such as bermuda and zoysiagrass, are best adapted in the southern Piedmont and much of the Tidewater area (Quantico through Farmville to Danville). Improved bermudagrasses such as 'Midiron' and 'Tufcote' are the better adapted varieties for lawns.

Tall fescue makes a tough lawn and is a good compromise in a transitional area and is the most extensively used species for lawns in this area. 'Ky 31' is the best variety and has consistently remained better than other tall fescue varieties in Virginia trials.

Publications office
Bulletin Room
Extension Division
Virginia Polytechnic Institute and State University
Blacksburg, Virginia 24061
Out of state requests: Yes.

NORTH CAROLINA

Soil and climate. The state of North Carolina conveniently divides into geographic thirds.

In the west around Asheville and all the area west of the Blue Ridge Mountains, use Kentucky bluegrass in the higher elevations. Bermudagrass, zoysiagrass, tall fescue, or Kentucky bluegrass is used at lower elevations.

For the Piedmont around Winston-Salem, Shelby, Hickory, and Eden, the main grasses are bermudagrass, zoysiagrass, and tall fescue. Centipedegrass can be grown in the warmest sections; Kentucky bluegrass in the coldest.

Along the Coastal Plain, use bermuda, centipede, or zoysiagrass on dry, well-drained soil and either carpetgrass or tall fescue in soil that tends to stay wet. Zoysia and centipedegrass are best in light shade. St. Augustinegrass is all right near the coast.

Lime. The abundant rainfall the state receives combined with the natural soil makes an acid soil. Lime (natural ground limestone is best) is almost always necessary.

Soil testing. Check with local County Extension Agent offices for mailing kits

and directions, or write:
Agronomic Division
North Carolina Department of Agriculture
Raleigh, North Carolina 27611
Recommended grasses. The best adapted grasses vary according to the three geographic regions.

Publications office
Publications Office
Department of Agricultural Information
Box 5037
State University Station
Raleigh, North Carolina 27607
Out of state requests: Yes.

of the best guides to a beautiful lawn in your area.

At the end of each state or group of states are lists of addresses you can write to for additional local information. Most states produce high-quality, pamphlets, brochures, or booklets that describe lawn growing.

The other addresses listed are for soil testing facilities. We've talked about the importance of soil tests throughout this book. In many cases the test is free, others may charge a nominal fee. Often, the most difficult part of getting your soil tested is knowing where to have it done.

About climate

Climate professionals use phrases such as "percent of sunshine" or "July days above 90°" the same as listed below. Here is what such words mean and how they relate to lawn growing.

Total inches rain. The average annual rainfall including snow, hail, and sleet. Rainfall, within a wide range of temperatures, is the most important environmental factor promoting or restricting growth of all plants. In some areas, excessive water is a problem. Caused by either too much rain or too slow drainage, wet soil will retard growth as surely as drought.

Rainfall can be plentiful in certain parts of the South but falls all at once or within a short season, thus is scant at other times of the year.

Too little rain is a more familiar problem. Soils that lose water rapidly by drainage (sandy soils) are more drought prone while lawns in heavy soils (clay) are less susceptible to short periods without rain.

Inches July/August. Referring to rainfall, this figure tells how much water falls naturally when the lawn needs it most, during the hot months of the year. A lawn's water requirements during summer is determined not only by grass type and soil, but also by the temperature and humidity.

July % of sunshine. Each day there is a certain amount of sunshine possible. This amount varies from the least on December 22 to the most on June 21. The actual number of sunshine hours also varies by latitude. In south Florida, December 22 is about 10½ hours and June 21 just less than 14. Percent of sunshine is figured by comparing the amount possible with the amount actually received. This figure indicates the number of cloudy, overcast days that occur in July.

July days above 90°F. The number of days in July when the temperature goes over 90°F. is one of the best guides to the grass type you should grow. It also indicates the stress a cool-season grass will be subjected to. The best temperatures for growth of the cool-season grasses such as Kentucky bluegrass are between 60 and 75°F. Warm-season grasses grow best when temperatures reach into the 80's and 90's.

Average maximum/minimum temperatures. These are the monthly averages of the daily temperature extremes. As such they are the best available guide to questions such as when to plant, water, and fertilize.

	TOTAL INCHES RAIN	INCHES JULY/AUG.	JULY % SUNSHINE	DEC. % SUNSHINE	JULY DAYS ABOVE 90°F.	AVERAGE MAXIMUM/MINIMUM TEMPERATURES											
						JAN.	FEB.	MARCH	APRIL	MAY	JUNE	JULY	AUG.	SEPT.	OCT.	NOV.	DEC.
VIRGINIA																	
Blacksburg	46	7.6	60	41	10	28/9	43/18	58/34	67/41	75/49	76/53	81/60	83/59	76/54	61/38	54/37	43/22
Charlottesville	44	9.9	64	41	21	33/17	49/22	63/41	72/46	80/56	81/60	93/67	89/64	82/62	66/45	55/40	44/27
Danville	43	8.6	63	50	24	37/17	51/23	66/39	76/46	82/56	84/60	95/68	92/67	85/61	66/43	60/40	48/27
Fredericksbg	40	9.2	68	52	26	36/13	54/25	65/38	75/42	82/53	86/58	95/66	92/65	85/59	69/44	55/40	46/28
Lynchburg	38	8.1	62	52	7	46/27	48/28	56/35	68/45	77/54	83/62	86/65	84/64	79/57	69/47	57/37	49/29
Norfolk	45	12	65	57	11	49/32	50/33	57/39	68/48	76/57	83/65	87/70	85/69	80/64	70/53	60/43	51/34
Richmond	43	11	65	51	13	47/28	50/29	58/35	70/45	78/54	85/63	88/67	87/66	81/59	71/47	61/37	49/29
Roanoke	39	7.9	61	41	9	46/27	48/28	56/34	68/44	76/53	83/60	86/64	85/63	79/56	70/46	58/36	47/28
NORTH CAROLINA																	
Asheville	45	9.4	60	57	3	48/27	51/28	58/33	69/42	77/51	82/59	84/63	81/62	78/55	69/44	58/34	49/28
Charlotte	43	8.5	69	58	11	52/32	55/33	62/39	73/49	80/57	86/65	88/69	87/68	82/62	73/50	62/40	52/32
Elizabeth City	50	9.9	70	55	17	40/22	54/31	64/44	74/51	79/57	83/63	90/69	89/70	85/66	69/51	65/47	54/35
Fayetteville	47	11	65	55	25	42/22	57/28	67/44	78/51	84/59	87/65	94/71	90/70	86/64	71/47	66/44	54/32
Greensboro	41	8.7	62	54	11	49/28	51/30	59/36	71/46	79/55	85/63	87/67	86/66	80/59	71/47	60/36	50/29
Raleigh	43	10	61	56	10	51/30	53/31	61/37	72/47	79/55	86/63	88/67	87/66	81/60	72/48	62/38	52/30
Rocky Mount	46	11	67	54	26	41/23	56/31	67/43	78/49	82/58	86/64	94/69	91/68	86/64	71/49	66/45	53/34
Wilmington	54	15	63	59	15	57/36	59/37	65/44	74/52	81/61	87/68	89/72	88/71	83/66	75/55	67/44	58/37

ARKANSAS

Soil and climate. If you draw an imaginary dividing line from the southwest to the northeast, you'll notice most of the west is mountainous while the east is lowlands. The soil of the lowlands is very fertile and holds water well. Here, droughts rarely cause damage. The soil of the uplands is in many cases severely eroded, and is of low fertility. Lawns in the uplands will suffer during hot and dry summers unless watered.

Rain is evenly distributed throughout the year. Spring rain is usually heaviest with May being, on the average, the wettest month. October is the driest month.

Lime needs to be added in most cases.

Soil testing. Contact your local County Extension Agent, or write:
Soil Testing Laboratory
Cooperative Extension Service
1201 McAlmont
P.O. Box 391
Little Rock, Arkansas 72203

Recommended grasses. Common bermudagrass is the most widely used lawngrass in Arkansas. Mowed and fertilized on a regular basis, it makes a very attractive lawn.

Improved bermudagrass is preferred by those desiring a very fine-textured, high-quality lawn. Use zoysiagrass in areas of 30 to 40 percent shade. They require less mowing and form dense, weed-free lawns.

Centipedegrass is slow to form a lawn, but can make an attractive turf. 'Oaklawn' is winter hardy throughout Arkansas.

Publications office
Cooperative Extension Service
Extension Publications Specialist
University of Arkansas
1201 McAlmont
P.O. Box 391
Litlte Rock, Arkansas 72203
Out of state requests: No.

OKLAHOMA

Soil and climate. The climate of Oklahoma is continental, meaning it has pronounced seasonal and geographic ranges in both temperature and rain.

Vast open plains make up the central and western sections. The western parts of the state are relatively cool and dry while the east is more hilly and the air more moist, with frequent showers.

Rain is fairly frequent throughout most of the state, though much less in the Panhandle.

The average length of the growing season varies from 180 days in the western part of Cimarron County, to 240 days in the extreme southeast.

Droughts and dust storms in the western parts of the state sometimes occur, but are rarely damaging outside the Panhandle.

Soil in the bottom lands is the most fertile and is used extensively for agriculture. Upland soil is most similar to soil of the Plains states.

Lime is usually needed. Determine by testing the soil. Use finely ground limestone.

Soil testing. Contact your local County Extension Office, or write:
Soil Testing Laboratory
Agronomy Department
Oklahoma State University
Stillwater, Oklahoma 74074

Recommended grasses. Bermudagrass is the lawngrass used most often. The common, seeded variety is most versatile, but some improved bermudagrasses are available.

The native buffalograss is well adapted to much of western Oklahoma. Buy seed that has been treated or else germination may be very slow and irregular.

Publications office
Central Mailing Service
Oklahoma State University
Cooperative Extension Office
Stillwater, Oklahoma 74704
Out of state requests: Yes.

TEXAS

Soil and climate. This state is so large and diverse that authorities have divided Texas into four regions of differing climates. In the southeast it's the Coastal Plains or East Texas Plains. This region extends from the coast to the Balcones Escarpment.

The north-central plains extend from the Black Lands westward to the Great Plains.

The Great Plains extend down from the north and northwest into Texas on the high ridge between the headwaters of the Canadian, Red, Brazos, and Colorado Rivers.

The last division is called the Trans-Pecos Mountain Area. It is a plateau lying west of Pecos Valley.

The growing season averages 185 days in the northern Panhandle, 230 days along the eastern and southern borders of the north-central divisions. From there to the coast, most of the counties have growing seasons over 300 days in length.

Rainfall averages over 50 inches in the east, but in the extreme west it averages less than 10 inches.

Soil in Texas varies in a similar degree. Generous amounts of organic matter are needed in most areas.

Lime is necessary in the eastern counties of the state.

Soil Testing
Texas Agricultural Extension Service
The Texas A&M University System
Soil Testing Laboratory
College Station, Texas 77843

Recommended grasses. Common bermudagrass and St. Augustinegrass are the most widely used and practical warm-season grasses for Texas.

Buffalograss is occasionally used in areas of the south and west where irrigation water is scarce.

Zoysiagrass and centipedegrass are grown in certain areas.

A bermudagrass lawn is common in Texas. Drought tolerance is good and the lawn is relatively trouble free. Common bermudagrass is easiest to plant and care for. Improved kinds, such as 'Tiflawn,' 'Texturf-10' and 'Tifdwarf' are available.

St. Augustinegrass is not as cold hardy or drought tolerant as bermudagrass, so should not be planted west or north of Ft. Worth. It grows satisfactorily east of a line from Vernon to Brady to Del Rio. 'Floratam,' selected through a combined effort of Florida and Texas agricultural scientists, has improved cold hardiness and pest resistance. St. Augustinegrass is sometimes confused with carpetgrass, which is rarely grown in Texas.

'Emerald' zoysiagrass is widely recommended for Texas. It is fine-leaved, dense-growing and dark green. 'Manilagrass' (*Zoysia matrella*) is fine textured but is not recommended, except in the southern parts of the state. 'Meyer' zoysiagrass accepts the cold.

Centipedegrass is adapted to sandy, well-drained soils in east, south, and central Texas.

Tall fescue is a good lawngrass for north and west Texas. It requires watering but makes a year-around green lawn. 'Kentucky 31' and 'Fawn' are improved varieties.

Almost exclusively cool-season lawns are used in El Paso, Amarillo, and in parts of the Panhandle.

Publications office
Texas Agricultural Extension Service
The Texas A&M University System
College Station, Texas 77843
Out of state requests: Yes.

	TOTAL INCHES RAIN	INCHES JULY/AUG.	JULY % SUNSHINE	DEC. % SUNSHINE	JULY DAYS ABOVE 90°F.	AVERAGE MAXIMUM/MINIMUM TEMPERATURES											
						JAN.	FEB.	MARCH	APRIL	MAY	JUNE	JULY	AUG.	SEPT.	OCT.	NOV.	DEC.

ARKANSAS

Blytheville	48	6.6	72	50	28	34/16	55/34	68/45	78/54	89/65	93/68	95/73	93/69	84/66	72/49	60/45	47/30
El Dorado	49	6.9	71	48	28	46/25	63/34	72/47	79/54	87/64	95/71	96/75	91/71	89/69	77/50	65/43	57/34
Fayetteville	44	9.5	74	56	21	34/13	54/27	61/40	72/51	80/58	88/65	90/70	87/68	82/63	71/45	59/40	50/27
Fort Smith	42	6.1	71	51	22	50/28	55/32	62/38	74/50	81/59	89/67	94/70	93/69	86/62	76/50	63/38	52/31
Harrison	51	8.1	74	55	19	33/14	53/29	63/40	73/51	80/59	87/66	89/70	87/68	80/63	70/48	56/41	51/27
Little Rock	49	6.4	71	48	22	50/29	54/32	62/39	73/50	81/58	89/67	93/70	93/69	86/61	76/49	62/38	52/31
Pine Bluff	51	5.6	71	48	25	40/20	59/33	69/43	78/52	86/63	92/69	94/72	92/71	89/67	77/49	63/42	53/31
Texarkana	37	5.3	73	50	25	45/27	61/38	69/48	77/56	84/64	91/71	93/74	93/73	89/70	79/55	65/48	57/37

OKLAHOMA

Altus	24	4.1	79	61	31	47/20	64/33	71/39	76/48	82/62	96/68	100/71	95/69	94/64	83/50	67/38	60/30
Enid	30	5.5	76	60	28	41/18	60/33	67/40	73/50	82/62	93/69	97/72	91/70	89/66	77/51	60/39	51/28
Lawton	30	4.7	79	60	29	44/21	61/33	68/42	75/52	82/62	93/69	97/71	94/71	92/65	80/49	67/42	55/28
Muskogee	42	6.3	75	55	28	38/18	58/33	66/44	76/55	83/62	92/70	97/74	91/72	85/68	73/52	60/44	52/31
Okla. City	31	5.2	75	59	22	48/26	53/30	60/36	72/49	79/58	87/67	93/70	92/70	85/61	74/51	61/37	51/29
Ponca City	36	8.4	76	60	25	36/15	56/31	64/39	72/51	80/60	89/68	95/71	88/69	81/63	73/48	57/39	48/25
Stillwater	32	6.4	75	59	27	39/16	58/29	65/39	74/50	83/61	91/69	95/72	91/71	86/65	77/48	63/40	53/27
Tulsa	37	6.4	72	54	23	47/26	52/30	60/37	72/50	79/58	87/67	93/71	93/70	85/62	75/51	61/38	50/29

TEXAS

Abilene	24	4.4	78	67	26	56/32	60/36	67/42	78/53	84/61	92/69	95/72	95/72	87/65	78/54	66/42	58/34
Amarillo	20	5.9	77	68	21	49/22	53/26	60/31	71/42	79/52	88/61	91/66	90/65	83/57	73/46	60/32	51/25
Austin	32	4.1	76	51	27	60/39	64/43	71/48	79/58	85/65	92/71	95/74	96/73	89/68	81/59	70/48	63/42
Brownsville	25	3.8	81	45	25	69/51	73/54	77/59	83/67	87/71	91/75	93/76	93/76	90/73	85/67	77/59	72/53
Corpus Christi	28	5.1	82	48	27	66/46	70/49	75/54	82/63	87/69	91/74	94/75	95/75	90/72	84/64	75/55	69/49
Dals.-Ft. Wrth.	32	4.1	75	52	27	56/34	60/38	67/43	76/54	83/62	91/70	95/74	96/74	88/67	79/56	67/44	59/37
Del Rio	17	2.2	77	58	27	63/38	69/43	76/49	85/59	90/66	96/72	99/74	98/74	92/68	83/59	72/47	65/39
El Paso	7.8	2.6	79	78	27	57/30	62/34	69/40	78/49	87/57	95/66	95/70	93/68	87/61	78/49	66/37	58/31
Galveston	42	8.8	72	49	3	59/48	61/51	66/56	73/65	80/72	85/77	87/79	88/79	85/75	78/68	69/58	63/51
Houston	48	8.5	67	65	26	63/41	66/45	72/50	79/59	86/66	91/71	94/73	94/72	90/68	83/58	73/49	66/43
Lubbock	18	4.1	74	75	21	53/25	57/28	64/34	75/45	82/54	91/64	92/67	91/65	84/58	75/47	63/34	55/27
Midland	13	3.3	79	65	25	58/29	62/33	69/39	79/49	86/58	93/67	95/69	94/69	88/63	79/52	67/39	60/32
San Angelo	18	2.7	77	60	27	59/34	63/37	71/43	80/54	86/62	93/70	97/72	97/72	88/65	80/55	68/42	61/35
San Antonio	28	4.1	75	52	28	62/40	66/43	72/49	80/59	86/65	92/72	96/74	96/73	90/69	82/59	71/48	66/42
Waco	31	3.3	75	52	28	57/37	61/40	69/46	78/57	84/64	92/72	96/75	97/75	89/68	80/58	69/46	60/39
Wichita Falls	27	3.9	79	60	28	53/29	58/34	66/39	77/51	85/60	94/69	99/72	99/72	90/64	79/53	66/40	56/32

ALABAMA

Soil and climate. Northeastern Alabama is a part of the Appalachian and Cumberland-Allegheny Plateau. Huntsville and Gadsden are cities in this area. The 200-day growing season is long compared to the United States average but is among the shortest in Alabama. Most of the soils here are loams, stony loams, sandy loams, silt loams, or clay loams.

Central Alabama is a rolling to hilly region. The growing season is as long as 240 days. A part of the Piedmont soil is mostly clay or clay loams.

Southern Alabama is highly influenced by the Gulf of Mexico. Around Mobile, the growing season is 265 days. This climate extends as far north as Chatom in Washington County. In the southern counties, heavy frosts are irregular due to the flow of cold air into low areas and down river valleys. In certain areas, the growing season will be shortened by this effect.
Lime is usually but not always needed. Through Coosa Valley and the Black Belts, the soil pH may be naturally close to ideal, but have the soil tested to be certain.
Soil testing
Soil Testing Laboratory
Auburn University
Auburn, Alabama 36830

Recommended grasses. North of Goodwater, Mantevallo, and Panda, some cool-season grasses such as Kentucky bluegrass and tall fescue are grown, especially at higher elevations.

Most lawns in the state, particularly south of Jackson, Frisco City, Evergreen, and Ozark, are warm-season grasses.

Publications office
Head, Administrative Services
Alabama Cooperative Extension Service
Auburn University
Auburn, Alabama 36380
Out of state requests: No.

MISSISSIPPI

Soil and climate. The two most important factors controlling Mississippi's climate are the North American continent itself to the north and west, and the Gulf of Mexico. Because the land is fairly level, topography has little influence on the climate. The highest land in the state near the northern border is less than 800 feet above sea level. The northeastern prairie belt and the Delta section (between the Tallahatchie-Yazoo Basin and the Mississippi River) are level and very fertile.
Lime. Much of the state receives more than 50 inches of rain each year, producing an acid soil. Lime should be added to most Mississippi soil before any money or time is spent on fertilizers. About 90 percent of the sandy soil in southern Mississippi need lime; more than two-thirds of Delta soil needs lime.
Soil testing. Check with your local County Extension Agent, or write:
Soil Testing
Box 5405
Mississippi State University
Mississippi 39762
Recommended grasses. Bermudagrass is the most common choice. Common bermudagrass can be seeded, but the improved 'Tif' bermudagrass varieties are finer textured.

Zoysiagrass is very slow to establish, but is attractive, and relatively problem free once it covers. 'Matrella' (same as manilagrass), 'Meyer,' and 'Emerald' zoysiagrass are used, and are good performers in moderate shade.

St. Augustinegrass is best for shady lawns, but lacks much cold tolerance.
Publications office
Chief Clerk
Mississippi State University
Oxford, Mississippi 49762
Mississippi 39762
Out of state requests: Yes.

LOUISIANA

Soil and climate. Louisiana's climate is determined by its subtropical latitude and nearness to the Gulf of Mexico.

Rainfall is evenly distributed with most falling in winter and mid-summer. On the average, between 45 and 60 inches of rain fall each year. As much as 86 inches falls on New Orleans.

The western two-thirds of Louisiana is part of the Coastal Plain. It is mostly level country with sandy soil. The highest elevation in the northwest section is 400 to 500 feet above sea level.

Most Louisiana soil is very acid and needs regular lime applications.

Lime refers, of course, to materials such as ground limestone, ground dolomite, or ground seashells. Besides raising the soil pH, lime adds essential calcium and magnesium nutrients. Lime makes other fertilizers more effective and improves the structure of heavy clay soils.

Soil testing
Soil Testing Laboratory
Department of Agronomy
Louisiana State University
Baton Rouge, Louisiana 70803

Recommended grasses. Centipedegrass is increasing in popularity in the Gulf Coast area. It will make a lawn in most any type soil (even poor) in the lower South.

Bermudagrass is adapted to well-drained, fertile soils with full exposure to the sun. It will persist, however, in both acid and over-limed soils. One tip: buy *hulled* bermudagrass seed.

Publications office

Publications Librarian
Room 192
Knapp Hall
Louisiana State University
Baton Rouge, Louisiana 70803
Out of state requests: Yes.

TENNESSEE

Soil and climate. Tennessee is in a region that receives abundant rainfall, about 50 inches on the average. As much as 80 inches has been measured in some of the mountain areas. Even with such rainfall, summer droughts are rather common.

Tennessee topography is varied. The east is mostly mountains but has broad fertile valleys. These East Tennessee valleys are similar to Maryland's Cumberland Valley, and the Shenandoah Valley in Virginia. The soil here is derived from limestone, sandstone, and shale and is very productive.

The Central Basin is a large section of central Tennessee that has rolling hills to 800 feet high. It is surrounded by hills several hundred feet higher called the Highland Rim. The Central Basin also has rich limestone soil, the same as the Kentucky bluegrass region of north-central Kentucky.
Lime is very often necessary. A soil test will tell if your soil needs lime or any other nutrients.
Soil testing
Soil Testing Laboratory
University of Tennessee
P.O. Box 11019
Nashville, Tennessee 37211

Recommended grasses. Kentucky bluegrass is widely adapted in Tennessee. The variety 'Windsor' has been tested and judged superior by local experts.

Bermudagrass is the most drought resistant. It does brown in winter, but is easily overseeded with ryegrass or other cool-season grass. Improved bermudagrass may perform well in Tennessee.
Publications office
Agricultural Extension Service
University of Tennessee
P.O. Box 1071
Knoxville, Tennessee 37901
Out of state requests: Yes.

	TOTAL INCHES RAIN	INCHES JULY/AUG.	JULY % SUNSHINE	DEC. % SUNSHINE	JULY DAYS ABOVE 90°F.	AVERAGE MAXIMUM/MINIMUM TEMPERATURES											
						JAN.	FEB.	MARCH	APRIL	MAY	JUNE	JULY	AUG.	SEPT.	OCT.	NOV.	DEC.
ALABAMA																	
Anniston	62	7.0	59	46	27	42/23	58/30	68/46	79/52	84/59	92/66	93/70	91/71	85/66	72/48	65/47	56/33
Birmingham	53	9.5	59	46	14	54/34	58/36	65/42	75/51	82/58	88/66	90/69	90/69	85/63	76/51	64/40	55/35
Enterprise	50	13	60	51	20	50/29	62/36	74/50	78/55	85/61	92/68	91/69	88/69	85/67	73/49	68/48	60/36
Huntsville	52	8.3	70	48	15	50/31	54/33	62/40	73/50	81/58	89/66	90/69	90/68	84/62	74/50	62/39	52/33
Mobile	67	16	61	51	24	61/41	64/44	69/49	78/58	85/64	90/71	90/73	91/72	86/68	80/58	69/47	63/43
Montgomery	50	8.5	63	50	20	58/37	61/40	68/45	77/54	84/61	89/69	90/71	91/71	86/65	78/53	67/43	59/38
Selma	52	8.8	64	49	27	48/28	63/36	72/50	82/54	88/62	92/70	94/23	92/72	89/69	76/51	69/50	61/39
Tuscaloosa	50	12	68	47	19	42/24	57/32	71/49	77/51	84/60	93/66	92/70	90/70	87/66	71/46	63/45	53/32
MISSISSIPPI																	
Biloxi	62	13	65	50	25	55/34	63/42	71/52	79/55	86/66	91/75	92/75	88/74	87/73	79/58	72/55	64/46
Greenwood	51	7.1	71	45	19	39/22	56/32	69/48	76/56	87/64	92/70	91/73	91/72	87/69	74/51	64/47	54/37
Hattiesburg	59	11	65	49	26	49/25	63/36	72/48	78/53	87/61	94/69	93/71	91/71	88/69	76/49	70/48	60/38
Jackson	49	7.8	62	47	24	58/36	62/38	69/43	78/53	85/60	91/68	93/71	93/70	88/64	80/51	68/42	60/37
Meridian	52	9.0	68	48	23	58/35	62/38	69/43	78/52	85/59	91/67	92/70	92/69	87/64	79/51	68/41	60/36
Natchez	54	7.6	71	48	28	49/31	65/40	75/52	79/56	87/64	94/71	93/73	90/73	88/70	78/54	69/50	62/41
Tupelo	54	7.9	71	47	26	40/20	61/26	70/42	79/48	86/56	93/64	94/70	94/67	88/64	74/44	64/44	54/33
Vicksburg	52	6.6	70	48	28	46/27	65/35	73/48	79/54	86/62	94/69	93/72	92/72	89/69	77/52	70/47	62/38
LOUISIANA																	
Alexandria	56	8.6	71	48	27	49/29	65/37	72/49	78/57	87/65	94/71	95/74	91/73	89/70	79/54	69/49	60/38
Baton Rouge	54	11	61	49	24	61/40	64/43	71/49	79/58	85/64	90/70	91/73	91/72	87/68	80/57	70/47	64/42
Lafayette	60	15	70	47	27	53/35	65/43	74/55	80/59	87/68	92/73	93/76	88/73	88/71	79/55	72/53	63/41
Lake Charles	55	11	71	47	22	62/43	65/45	70/50	78/59	84/66	90/72	91/74	91/73	88/69	82/58	71/49	64/44
Monroe	50	7.1	72	48	19	47/28	65/40	73/49	78/56	87/64	94/71	91/73	90/71	88/68	77/50	65/45	56/38
Natchitoches	50	6.0	72	49	30	49/28	65/37	73/48	79/55	88/64	95/70	96/73	92/72	90/70	80/53	69/48	61/37
New Orleans	57	12	58	53	20	62/43	65/46	70/51	78/59	85/65	90/71	90/73	91/73	87/70	80/60	70/50	64/45
Shreveport	45	5.6	73	53	25	57/39	60/41	67/46	77/56	84/63	90/70	93/73	94/72	88/67	79/56	67/48	59/39
TENNESSEE																	
Bristol	41	8.7	60	43	5	46/27	49/28	57/34	68/44	77/53	84/61	86/64	85/63	80/57	70/45	57/34	47/28
Chattanooga	52	8.3	61	42	16	50/30	53/32	61/38	73/48	81/56	87/64	89/68	89/67	83/60	73/48	61/37	51/31
Knoxville	46	7.9	61	38	8	49/32	52/33	60/39	72/49	80/57	86/65	88/68	87/67	82/61	72/50	59/39	50/33
Memphis	49	6.9	73	50	21	49/32	53/34	61/41	73/52	81/61	89/68	92/71	91/70	84/63	75/51	61/40	52/34
Nashville	46	7.0	65	41	15	48/29	51/31	59/38	71/49	80/57	87/66	90/69	89/68	83/60	73/49	59/38	50/31
Oak Ridge	53	9.5	61	38	10	47/29	50/30	59/36	70/46	79/54	85/63	87/66	87/65	81/59	71/47	58/36	48/30
Jackson	49	7.0	72	49	21	32/15	52/24	66/42	75/51	84/60	88/65	92/71	89/68	84/65	70/44	60/42	47/29

SOUTH CAROLINA

Soil and climate. The general climatic patterns are very similar to those of North Carolina. However, the western mountains are not nearly as extensive, and the more southern latitude means a warmer climate.

South Carolina is divided into the two regions of the Piedmont and the Coastal Plain. The border of the two regions is roughly from the eastern boundary of Aiken County through central Chesterfield County, to the North Carolina border.

On the average, rainfall is heaviest in July, and least in November. Thunderstorms are frequent in summer.

The shortest season in the state is just under 200 days. Along the southern coast, the growing season averages 300 days.

Soils of the Piedmont and Coastal Plain are essentially the same as described for North Carolina.

Soil testing. Sample boxes and record sheets are available from local County Extension Agent offices, or write:
Soil Testing Laboratory
Clemson University
Clemson, South Carolina 29631

Recommended grasses. Bahiagrass is well adapted in the Sandhills vicinity as well as in most of the rest of the South Carolina Coastal Plain.

Common bermudagrass is one of the most widely used grasses. Improved types of bermudagrass such as 'Tifgreen,' 'Tiflawn,' and 'Tifway' are often planted (see page 16).

Carpetgrass is useful where soil is too wet or infertile for bermudagrass, even though it does not make the most handsome lawn.

Centipedegrass is frequently used in the Piedmont, Sandhills, and Coastal Plains areas.

St. Augustinegrass is best, in sun or some shade, confined to the Coastal Plain.

Of the zoysiagrasses, 'Meyer' is the easiest to maintain, 'Emerald' is the most beautiful, and 'Matrella' is the most widely adapted.

Tall fescue is the most heat tolerant of all the cool-season grasses.

Some of the improved Kentucky bluegrasses, such as 'Nugget,' 'Adelphi', or 'Baron,' are useful in partially shaded sites.

Use annual ryegrass or a premium cool-season mixture to overseed dormant bermudagrass.

Publications office
Agricultural Publications
Department of Public Relations
Clemson University
Clemson, South Carolina 29631
Out of state requests: Yes.

GEORGIA

Soil and climate. The climate in Georgia is controlled by the altitude, latitude, and proximity to the ocean. The state essentially has a warm, humid climate, modified considerably by the higher mountains in the northern parts of the state (from Atlanta to the Tennessee border).

More than half the state is included in the Coastal Plain. The soil is sandy and the land fairly level. Piedmont soil is mostly clay and clay loams, but some have a sandy surface in the top few inches. They will all be acid and not terribly fertile, though certainly capable of good production.

Lime is necessary in most cases, especially for new lawns.

Soil testing
Soil Testing and Plant Analysis Laboratory
2400 College Station Road
Athens, Georgia 30601

Recommended grasses. Common bermudagrass is by far the most prevalent lawngrass in Georgia.

Dr. Glen Burton of the Georgia Coastal Plains Experiment Station developed several of the most-used improved bermudagrasses such as 'Tiflawn,' 'Tifway,' 'Tifgreen,' and 'Tifdwarf.'

Tall fescue is the most popular grass in the mountain and upper Piedmont areas.

Carpetgrass is useful in wet soils, not infrequent in the central and southern parts of the state.

St. Augustinegrass is the best shade-tolerant grass for most parts of Georgia.

Of the zoysiagrass, 'Emerald' is most attractive and the best overall for Georgia.

Publications office
Extension Editor — Publications
University of Georgia
Athens, Georgia 30602
Out of state requests: Yes.

FLORIDA

Soil and climate. The entire state of Florida is included within the Coastal Plain. Its climate is dominated most directly by the surrounding seas — no point in the state is more than 60 miles from the coast. Florida is very flat. The highest point in the state is 325 feet above sea level; the average elevation is somewhat less.

The soil is variable. Along the coast it tends to be sandy pinelands and marshes. Darker and more fertile soil occurs towards the interior. Muck soil reclaimed from the Everglades is among the most fertile. In a few areas, the soil is clay-like.

Lime is often necessary, but some soil is too "sweet." Check soil pH with a soil test.

Soil testing. Check with a County Extension Agent, or write:
Soil Testing Laboratory
University of Florida
Gainsville, Florida 32601

Recommended grasses. The grasses of Florida include St. Augustine, centipede, bermuda, zoysia, carpet, and bahiagrass.

Bahiagrass is native to Brazil and better adapted to central Florida than anywhere else in the South.

Improved varieties of bahiagrass are available. 'Argentine' is most popular for lawns. 'Pensacola' is used along highways. Common bahiagrass is little used. Mole crickets are a major problem in bahiagrass.

St. Augustinegrass makes a beautiful lawn in many situations, especially in shady areas. It is the most popular lawngrass in the state. A good insect and disease program is necessary to keep it in good shape. The variety 'Bitter Blue,' low growing and dense, was developed on the lower east coast. It has an attractive color but will not tolerate heavy traffic.

'Floratine' is similar to 'Bitter Blue' in many respects but is even more dense. It can be mowed as close as ½ inch.

'Floratam' has shown some resistance to both chinch bugs and SAD disease (see page 77), but does not tolerate much shade.

Bermudagrass, especially the improved types like 'Tifgreen' and 'Tiflawn,' will make a most attractive lawn but will require very high maintenance.

'Emerald' zoysiagrass is often recommended for Florida gardeners. It will take a lot of shade, but is slow to cover.

Centipedegrass makes a good, low maintenance lawn but may be seriously damaged by nematodes — especially in sandy soil. For this reason, it is rarely recommended for planting south of Orlando, where sandy soil is more commonplace. Ground pearls are also a problem.

Publications office
Bulletin Room
Cooperative Extension Service
University of Florida
Gainsville, Florida 32601
Out of state requests: Yes.

For special tips on Florida lawns see page 93.

	TOTAL INCHES RAIN	INCHES JULY/AUG.	JULY % SUNSHINE	DEC. % SUNSHINE	JULY DAYS ABOVE 90° F.	AVERAGE MAXIMUM/MINIMUM TEMPERATURES											
						JAN.	FEB.	MARCH	APRIL	MAY	JUNE	JULY	AUG.	SEPT.	OCT.	NOV.	DEC.

SOUTH CAROLINA

	TOTAL INCHES RAIN	INCHES JULY/AUG.	JULY % SUNSHINE	DEC. % SUNSHINE	JULY DAYS ABOVE 90° F.	JAN.	FEB.	MARCH	APRIL	MAY	JUNE	JULY	AUG.	SEPT.	OCT.	NOV.	DEC.
Aiken	46	9.8	63	51	28	47/27	62/30	72/48	81/51	87/59	95/67	96/70	90/69	87/67	74/50	72/48	60/37
Anderson	40	3.7	61	50	28	41/22	59/27	69/46	79/54	85/62	91/68	95/73	91/72	85/68	72/51	65/49	54/36
Charleston	52	15	67	59	15	60/37	62/39	68/45	76/53	83/61	88/68	89/71	89/71	84/66	77/55	68/44	61/38
Clemson	51	9.4	60	52	26	41/20	56/26	66/42	76/49	82/58	89/63	93/68	89/67	84/64	70/45	61/43	51/31
Columbia	46	11	64	60	20	57/34	60/35	66/42	77/51	84/60	90/67	92/70	91/69	85/63	78/51	67/41	58/34
Georgetown	51	13	65	55	21	49/27	62/30	71/47	80/52	83/61	90/67	93/72	89/71	87/68	75/52	72/50	62/40
Greenville	47	8.2	59	54	11	52/33	54/35	62/40	72/50	80/58	86/66	88/69	87/68	81/62	72/51	62/40	52/33
Greenwood	46	8.3	62	51	27	43/20	57/23	68/41	78/48	83/55	91/63	95/68	90/67	85/63	71/45	65/41	54/30
Florence	46	10	64	54	24	43/24	59/30	68/47	79/53	84/60	88/66	94/72	88/70	87/68	72/48	67/45	56/35
Orangeburg	48	11	63	54	27	44/24	59/30	70/46	80/52	87/59	92/66	97/70	89/68	86/65	71/46	61/44	55/33
Spartanburg	46	5.1	60	50	26	42/23	58/30	69/44	77/51	83/55	89/64	94/66	88/67	84/63	72/47	64/43	54/31
Sumter	47	11	64	60	27	46/26	62/33	72/48	82/54	86/61	91/66	96/71	90/68	88/65	75/51	71/48	51/37

GEORGIA

	TOTAL INCHES RAIN	INCHES JULY/AUG.	JULY % SUNSHINE	DEC. % SUNSHINE	JULY DAYS ABOVE 90° F.	JAN.	FEB.	MARCH	APRIL	MAY	JUNE	JULY	AUG.	SEPT.	OCT.	NOV.	DEC.
Athens	51	8.8	62	51	15	53/33	56/35	63/40	74/50	82/58	88/66	89/69	89/68	83/62	74/51	63/40	54/34
Atlanta	48	8.4	62	50	7	51/33	54/35	61/41	71/51	79/59	85/67	86/69	86/69	81/63	72/52	62/41	53/34
Augusta	43	9.3	63	51	19	58/34	60/36	67/42	77/51	84/59	90/67	91/70	90/69	85/63	77/51	67/40	59/34
Columbus	51	10	65	51	20	58/36	61/38	67/43	77/52	85/60	90/67	91/70	91/70	86/65	77/53	67/42	59/36
Macon	44	8.2	64	56	21	59/37	62/39	68/45	78/53	86/61	91/68	92/71	92/70	87/65	78/53	68/42	60/37
Rome	53	8.2	66	48	17	52/30	56/32	63/37	74/47	82/55	82/63	90/67	90/66	85/60	75/47	63/36	53/31
Savannah	51	14	63	55	19	61/39	64/40	69/46	78/54	85/62	89/69	91/71	90/71	85/67	78/56	69/45	62/39
Tifton	47	11	63	54	28	48/28	61/34	71/52	80/56	86/63	98/69	93/72	89/71	87/69	76/50	69/50	60/37

FLORIDA

	TOTAL INCHES RAIN	INCHES JULY/AUG.	JULY % SUNSHINE	DEC. % SUNSHINE	JULY DAYS ABOVE 90° F.	JAN.	FEB.	MARCH	APRIL	MAY	JUNE	JULY	AUG.	SEPT.	OCT.	NOV.	DEC.
Apalachicola	57	16	64	57	6	61/46	63/48	68/54	75/61	82/68	86/74	87/75	88/75	85/72	78/63	69/53	63/48
Daytona Bch.	50	13	60	59	16	69/48	70/49	74/53	80/59	85/65	88/70	90/72	89/73	87/72	81/65	75/55	70/49
Fort Meyers	54	17	64	65	22	75/52	76/53	80/57	85/62	89/66	90/72	91/74	91/74	90/73	85/67	80/59	76/54
Jacksonville	54	15	60	56	23	65/44	67/46	72/50	79/57	85/64	88/70	90/72	90/72	86/70	79/62	71/51	66/45
Key West	40	8.6	77	73	14	76/66	77/65	79/70	82/74	85/76	88/79	89/80	89/80	88/79	84/75	80/71	76/67
Lakeland	49	15	61	63	21	70/51	72/52	76/56	82/62	87/67	90/71	90/73	90/73	88/72	82/66	76/57	71/52
Miami	60	14	79	54	8	76/59	77/59	79/63	83/67	85/71	88/74	89/75	90/76	88/75	85/71	80/64	77/60
Orlando	51	15	61	60	24	70/50	72/51	76/56	81/61	88/66	89/71	90/73	90/73	88/72	82/66	76/57	71/51
Pensacola	64	14	57	49	17	61/43	64/45	69/51	77/59	84/66	87/72	90/74	90/74	86/70	80/60	70/49	63/44
Tallahassee	62	16	60	56	22	64/41	66/43	72/48	80/56	87/63	90/70	91/72	90/70	87/69	81/58	71/46	65/41
Tampa	49	16	61	62	19	71/50	72/52	76/56	82/62	87/67	90/72	90/74	90/74	89/73	84/65	77/56	72/51
W. Palm Bch.	62	13	65	67	15	75/56	76/56	79/60	83/65	86/69	88/73	90/74	90/74	88/75	84/70	79/62	76/57

Lawn calendar

Temperatures control the timetable but not the calendar. However, we must use the calendar to express time. The South is a diverse area. For example, temperatures in the South for the month of March range from 53°F. in Lexington, Kentucky to 80°F. in Miami, Florida.

Climate comparisons of 20 cities:

cities	number of days growing season	average last frost	average first frost
Roanoke, VA	187	4/15	10/15
Lubbock, TX	205	4/10	10/30
Tulsa, OK	216	3/30	10/30
Louisville, KY	220	3/30	11/8
Knoxville, TN	220	3/30	11/8
Baltimore, MD	234	3/20	11/12
Raleigh, NC	237	3/17	11/12
Memphis, TN	237	3/15	11/7
Birmingham, AL	241	3/15	11/13
Little Rock, AK	244	3/10	11/11
Atlanta, GA	244	3/15	11/14
Dallas, TX	249	3/17	11/22
Norfolk, VA	254	3/15	11/24
Augusta, GA	260	3/8	11/17
Shreveport, LA	272	3/1	12/3
Savannah, GA	291	2/24	12/6
Charleston, SC	294	3/1	11/10
New Orleans, LA	302	2/10	12/10
Corpus Christi, TX	335	1/12	12/20
Miami, FL	365	—	—

The high and low temperatures for each month, total inches rainfall, July-August rainfall, percent of July and December sunshine, and days in July above 90°F., are listed for 111 towns beginning on page 80. Let them be your timetable guide.

The many lawn climates of the South

The South is big. We're talking about

1. South Atlantic Coast influence.
2. Gulf Coast.
3. Arid regions of the South.
4. Cooler northern regions.

We're talking about growing days (days between frosts) varying from 187 to 365.

The important regions in the southeast are:
1. Coastal Plain.
2. Piedmont.
3. Mountains.

January-February

Winter weeds: In areas of the South where weather warms up early, pre-emergent treatments for crabgrass, spurweed, and annual bluegrass are applied about one month before seeds germinate (see crabgrass control under March listing). You can also spot-treat wild garlic as it emerges with 2,4-D, or other recommended chemicals.

Fertilizer: In the warmest areas of the South where a lawn may stay green all year, bermuda, bahia, St. Augustine and zoysiagrass can benefit from the boost they'll get from an early feeding.

Insects: If it's warm enough to apply fertilizer where you live, then grubs that overwintered in the soil should be near the surface, where they can be controlled. Get rid of them now if you missed the chance last fall.

March-April

Watch for the first signs of green growth as bermuda, St. Augustine, centipede, carpet or bahiagrass begin to grow faster. It can come as early as January or February in the mildest sections and it may not come until April in the upper South. When spring does arrive, temperatures about 70°F. signal the opening of the lawn season.

Mowing low: Set your mower to cut just above the new grass blades to warm the soil and expose new growth to more light. If you had a temporary winter lawn of ryegrass or fescue, low mowing will discourage its growth and give your permanent lawn a chance to take over.

Fertilizer: You can follow our monthly program for feeding as outlined on these pages or make your own schedule based on the requirements and needs of your specific grasses. Figure that 1,000 square feet of lawn needs the following amounts of nitrogen per year: 4 to 6 pounds for St. Augustinegrass, 6 to 12 pounds for the improved bermudagrasses, 4 to 6 pounds for bahia, 3 pounds for carpet and centipedegrass, and 4 to 6 pounds for zoysiagrass. For more information, see the section on fertilizing, page 52. Not all warm-season grasses require fertilizer at this time. Feeding of bermuda and St. Augustinegrass lawns is needed if they were

not fed last month. During the month of April both carpet and centipedegrass should also be fed. Kentucky bluegrass, fescue, and ryegrass require spring feeding if a heavy application wasn't applied in the fall. Along with the green leaf growth, tillers, runners, and underground rhizomes develop rapidly in the rush of spring growth.

Patching: Repair winter damage with pieces of sod, sprigs, or plugs. You may want to use seed if you have Kentucky bluegrass, other cool-season grasses, or bahiagrass.

Sodding: A practice that can actually be done at any time during the growing season, it is normally done during spring and fall.

Crabgrass: You can do your lawn a favor if crabgrass or annual bluegrass was a problem last summer. Seeds left over from last year sprout when temperatures reach 65° to 70°F. continually for four to five days. To stop their germination, use a pre-emergent barrier a month before seeds begin to germinate. This should be about February in the mildest areas, in mid-March in the Coastal Plain, and the end of March in the upper South. Pre-emergent chemicals like Tupersan should be used if you plan on doing any spring seeding. They kill crabgrass but not most lawn seeds. Read the label to be sure.

Disease: The cool, moist weather of spring favors development of several fungus diseases. Cottony blight on ryegrass and leaf spot are among those present now and again in the fall. Dollar spot can occur anytime until late summer, especially with high humidity and temperatures of 80°F. (See diseases, page 73.)

May

Planting: Warming weather makes May and June prime months for planting a warm-season grass lawn. You can plant as late as July, but later plantings may not have time to establish before cooler weather. Common bermudagrass lawns can be started from seed, but improved bermuda, St. Augustine, and most of the other warm-season grasses are started vegetatively. Be sure to control weeds so that the lawn can establish quickly without competition for light, water, and nutrients.

Dethatching: Scrutinize established lawns for buildup of thatch — particularly in bermuda and St. Augustinegrass. Thatch blocks out air and water, and fosters pests and diseases. Thin it out with a heavy rake if the area is small, rent a power rake (renovator), or hire a lawn service company for larger lawns.

Fertilizer: This month feed warm-season grasses except carpet and centipede. If a lawn stays yellow in spite of feedings, the problem may be a shortage of iron called chlorosis. The condition, common to centipede and other Southern grasses, can be corrected with sprays containing iron. This is another time for a light application of fertilizer on bluegrass, fescue or ryegrass. They will make good growth before the hot weather of summer slows them down.

Broadleaf weeds: Blooming dandelions are a sure sign of weeds, but plantain, sheep sorrel, and many others that are less obvious are just as troublesome. Most weeds grow well at 70°F. and are most vulnerable to herbicides while still young. In addition, weed killers formulated for their control are most effective in warm but not hot weather. If tough-to-kill weeds like oxalis and spurge are pestering your lawn, see pages 60 to 65 for directions on their control.

June

A lawn that has received the right care should look like a masterpiece this month, though cool-season lawns begin to slump with the onset of hot weather (proper watering will help keep them looking their best).

Fertilizer: Bermuda and zoysiagrass need fertilizer this month. Bluegrass, fescue, and ryegrass remain slow growing until fall brings cooling weather.

Insects: Chinch bugs are a part of life to St. Augustinegrass. The bugs thrive in the lawn's sunniest, driest spots. Infested patches turn yellow, then brown. Follow this test to make sure that the problem is caused by chinch bugs: Start near the edge of the damaged area and push a bottomless can down into the lawn; keep it filled with water for about five minutes. If chinch bugs are there, they will float to the surface. Treat the whole lawn as chinch bugs spread quickly. Another likely June pest is the sod webworm. You'll probably notice adult moths first — fluttering close to the lawn at dusk, laying eggs. Two weeks later, the worms hatch and start feeding on grass blades at night. To confirm their presence, examine dead patches for larvae. Look for them during the day; they curl up in the thatch of the turf.

Armyworms also feed on lawns, but they're twice as big as webworms, and feed in broad daylight. Control is the same as for sod webworms. It is best to apply these insecticides in the late afternoon or evening.

Grassy weeds: If you have crabgrass in your lawn, it's big enough to be noticeable by now. You can stop adolescent and mature growth with post-emergent annual grass controls.

Other grassy weeds become prominent this month. Dallisgrass and nutgrass are hard to get rid of and may require monthly applications for control. In June, you may also notice *Poa annua*, (annual bluegrass). It's light green and pretty enough in spring, but when hot weather comes it sets seed and dies in unsightly patches. There is not much you can do about it now: Wait until August and September.

July-August

Hot weather calls for some changes in a lawn maintenance routine. Keep watching for sod webworm and chinch bugs. Continue feeding as needed for your type of lawn. Bermuda and zoysiagrass favor feeding in both July and August. Bahia, carpet, St. Augustine, and centipedegrass can skip the August application. Do not overfeed. Excessive feeding favors sod webworm and army worms.

Mowing: Raise mowing height to provide more shade for roots. This is important if you want to keep a cool-season grass from going dormant.

Watering: Watering is the most important job for these months. How much you water depends on your kind of soil and climate, but the general rules of watering deeply and infrequently hold true under most conditions.

Disease: The most likely summer lawn disease is brown patch. Warm humid weather favors its development. To keep it from spreading, especially if favorable weather continues, mow, rake, feed, and water thoroughly. An adequate safeguard against brown patch is simply good maintenance.

September

Even as weather cools, summer routines should be kept in mind — feeding, chinch bug control, disease prevention, watching for sod webworm.

Fertilizing: It is particularly important to continue regular feeding — the last feeding of the year (except in the

Deep South) is an important one for St. Augustine, carpet, Bahia and centipede grass. Bermudagrass can also take another dose. For Kentucky bluegrass, fescue, and ryegrass, the months ahead are the most important feeding times of the year — they are building up root systems and storing reserves while producing less top growth than they did in the spring.

Planting: It's the best time of the year to start a cool-season lawn. Warm temperatures will germinate seeds, and, with the coming of cool weather and fall rains, you'll have to do less watering and the lawn will establish quickly.

Grassy weeds: Now is the chance to begin a campaign against *Poa annua*. The idea is to prevent seeds from sprouting this fall. Early this month, apply a pre-emergent herbicide labeled for this purpose. Apply it again next spring.

October-November

Fertilizing: In early fall, feed bermuda, zoysia, bahia, and St. Augustine one last time to build strength for winter, and help get it off to a fast start in spring. This is the most important feeding of the year for a cool-season lawn. Your lawn will have more strength in winter, a more vigorous root system and start stronger early next spring.

Overseeding: If your bermudagrass lawn goes dormant in the upper South, you may want to overseed with ryegrass or fescue.

An alternative is to color the lawn (see pages 92 to 93). Rake the lawn and mow closely before seeding. Sow seeds and keep moist until germination.

Broadleaf weeds: The return of cool weather gives you another crack at broadleaf weeds. A good many kinds start out in fall and are at their most vulnerable stage. Remember, broadleaf herbicides work best in warm (not hot) weather.

Good timing

Timing of course is an important part of lawn care. But it's just one of the important steps to a good lawn. You must put all the steps together. 1. Use adapted grasses. 2. Mow regularly at the correct height. 3. Fertilize according to what's best for the adapted grass. 4. Kill broadleaf weeds at the best time. 5. Prevent crabgrass if necessary. 6. Keep insects under control. 7. Remove thatch when necessary. 8. Protect against diseases that kill the lawn. 9. Irrigate to keep the lawn in good condition.

Lawn tips

A book about lawns is never complete. Here are some miscellaneous tips we've pulled out of previous chapters to serve as handy information in a concentrated form.

Trees in the lawn

The main cause of damage to trees in the lawn results from lawn mowers bumping the trunk. Any wound in the bark is an invitation to insects and disease. Three wooden stakes placed about one foot from the trunk can be used to protect young trees.

Grass growing against the trunk of a young tree can severely retard the tree's growth, even if additional water and fertilizer are applied. A 30-inch in diameter ring of mulch around the tree can give it a good start. Keep mulch away from the trunk.

Grade changes can kill many trees. Piling soil around the trunk can suffocate surface roots. Removing soil either damages roots or exposes them to drying. During the establishment of a lawn, any grade changes around trees should be gradual. Changes of more than a couple of inches require the use of retaining walls or dry wells, which are best extended to the dripline of the tree.

Some trees that are especially adapted to growing in southern lawns include:

Carya illinoinensis	Pecan
Cercis canadensis	Redbud
Chionanthus spp.	Fringe tree
Cornus spp.	Dogwood
Crataegus spp.	Hawthorne
Koelreuteria spp.	Golden-rain tree
Magnolia spp.	Magnolia
Pyrus spp.	Pear
Pinus spp.	Pine
Quercus spp.	Oak

Instead of a lawn, ground covers can be grown under trees. If the shade is more than 50 percent, ground covers are a better solution than turf.

Changing grade

Even after a lawn is established, you may want to change the grade to correct water run-off or level high and low areas. Grass will grow with the addition of small amounts of sand, organic matter, and top soil. You will find change of grade is simpler if you go at it gradually, adding or subtracting a little fill at a time.

Leaves on the lawn

There are leaves that easily blow away and there are leaves that are big and determined to stay on your lawn. Some trees drop their leaves in a short time while others seem to drop forever. Regardless of when and how they fall, rake them up and add them to the compost pile. They will decay faster if they're shredded. Leaves do not act like a blanket to keep the grass warm. They actually smother the lawn, especially when it's wet, thus depriving the grass of light.

Lawn clippings as a mulch

If you use lawn clippings as a compost or mulch in the vegetable garden, take care that the lawn clippings are free of 2,4-D, and other broadleaf weed killers. 2,4-D affects plants in various ways. Continuous mulching of tomatoes with treated clippings has resulted in distorted plants. Let clippings treated with 2,4-D settle into the lawn, or discard.

Washboard effect

Turfgrass areas regularly cut with a power mower may develop wave-like ridges running at right angles to the direction of mowing. Alternating directions of cut will help correct these ridges.

Mow less often

Recently tested growth regulators have displayed the ability to slow lawngrass growth for 5 to 8 weeks.

Trees in the lawn require special care. One of the most important requirements is a ring of open soil or mulch around the tree trunk. Grass growing against the trunk of young trees can retard the tree's growth.

Lawns are mowed only half as often when the chemicals are used.

Several difficulties prevent marketing for home use at this time: 1. The regulators work best only on single-grass lawns. 2. Slowed growth may favor weeds and disease. 3. Weather, stage of growth, fertility status, and time of application all effect results. 4. Improper application can cause damage to the lawn. Presently available growth regulators are best adapted for difficult or impossible mowing situations; along fences, walls, or on steep, unmowable slopes, for example.

Paving block lawns

Concrete paving blocks combined with turfgrass will produce a new kind of multi-use lawn area. A paving block lawn can be used as a driveway, parking area, or pathway. They are similar in appearance to oversized checkerboards, with alternating squares of supportive blocks and planting holes. An average-sized block covers about three square feet. Standard concrete building blocks can also be used.

Planting a lawn with paving blocks is a simple operation. If the proposed area will be required to support heavy weight, such as a driveway, a solid base for the blocks should be pre-pared. The paving blocks are placed in position side by side, and the holes filled with a quality soil. Seed or sod plugs can then be planted, the same as for any new lawn. After establishment, the weight of vehicles or heavy foot traffic is supported by the blocks, not the turf.

There are many advantages to this type of lawn. They are naturally more attractive than bare soil or artificial surface, and are cooler and produce less glare. During the rainy season water runoff is less due to the lawn's greater absorption qualities.

Different grass types produce different effects. A vertically growing grass such as tall fescue will obscure the blocks completely. A horizontal grass such as bermuda will stay low, allowing some of the paving block to remain exposed, providing a textured pattern.

The cost of a paving block lawn will of course vary with the situation. As a general rule, however, it should be the same or even less than poured concrete.

New sod lawns

Prevent tearing corners of sod that has not yet rooted by mowing at a 45 degree angle to the edge. Such a mowing pattern has less tendency to lift sod.

Lawn colorants

Many of the objections that were expressed when colorants were first introduced are no longer valid. Quality colorants will not rub off, walk off or wash off. They have become fade-proof, non-toxic and long wearing. The first application of colorant should be made immediately following the first killing frost. To prepare the turf, mow the grass to one inch or less, then mow at right angles to the first pass to provide as even a turf as possible. All clippings, litter and debris should be removed before the colorant is applied. Mix colorant according to directions on the label. That ratio will vary, depending on the color intensity desired. One gallon of colorant will normally cover 4,000 square feet of turf. The turf should be colorized twice, the second application made at right angles to the first to assure uniform color.

Treat the cause, not the symptom

If a trouble spot develops, search, then treat the cause, not the symptom. Here are some examples:

A dry spot that appears repeatedly in the lawn may result from a lack of organic matter, or improper grading.

Turf block lawns provide a cool, attractive alternative to concrete or asphalt driveways. The weight of the car is supported by the blocks, and not the sod.

A very important "tip" is aeration. It eliminates compaction, and allows air, water, and fertilizer to get to the root zone. A manual model works well on small lawn areas; use a power model for large lawns.

Not enough depth to the soil above bedrock, or buried concrete or debris will also cause drying.

Moss: If you have a problem with moss, there are temporary cures, but for a permanent solution, look for the cause. Moss is usually the result of improper drainage and shade, not soil acidity. Other factors contributing to moss are poor air circulation and insufficient light, which slow the evaporation of water from the soil.

Powdered copper sulfate at three tablespoons per 1,000 square feet or ammonium sulfate at 10 pounds per 1,000 square feet are chemical controls which may be used. Also, fertilizers containing ferrous and ferric ammonium sulfate will control moss. Be aware, however, this amount of ammonia sulfate may furnish too much nitrogen for cool-season grasses if applied in late spring.

Mushrooms: After prolonged periods of wet weather, you may notice mushrooms coming up in the lawn. This often indicates the presence of construction debris or old tree roots and stumps that are decaying below the surface. It may be years after construction before the mushrooms appear. There is no effective chemical control for these fungi and they cause no damage to the turf. However, if you feel they are unsightly and poisonous, remove them with the lawn mower or a bamboo rake.

Moles: A single mole can range over several acres, digging several thousand feet of tunnels. The structure of the surface tunnels and the temporary way in which they are used makes mole control difficult. Gases introduced into these tunnels are ineffective because they will quickly diffuse through the thin overhead sod covering. Since moles are primarily carniverous, it is difficult to poison them. The most practical control is to trap the animal, which can be very time consuming, or to remove their food supply so that they migrate elsewhere. Until their primary food source, grubs and earthworms, is eliminated, moles will continue to move in to feed. If you have moles, the best solution is to treat for grubs.

Dethatching

The southern grasses respond differently to dethatching by vertical mowing (see ages 57 to 59). We quote the Texas Agricultural Extension Service bulletin MP-1180:

"Bermudagrass and bluegrass respond favorably to vertical mowing, but care should be taken with non-rhizomatous turfgrasses such as St. Augustinegrass. If the St. Augustinegrass is not well-rooted, serious thinning can occur as a result of vertical mowing. Equipment blades should be spaced 1½ to 2 inches apart and should not penetrate too deeply into St. Augustinegrass turf. Vertical mowing can best be accomplished in early spring, just prior to the initiation of new growth. Fall vertical mowing of bermudagrass may cause an increase in clover, annual bluegrass, and other winter weeds. Likewise, early summer dethatching of Kentucky bluegrass may increase the infestation of crabgrass."

Centipedegrass decline

Centipedegrass is hardy in areas of the south from as far west as Galveston, Texas, to Baton Rouge, Louisianna and Charleston, South Carolina. We quote from the University of Georgia leaflet No. 177:

"Centipedegrass is adapted to south Georgia and survives as far north as Athens or Atlanta during most years. Centipede is one of the prevalent lawngrasses of middle and south Georgia. Its popularity is due to ease of establishment and low main-

When you see mushrooms in the lawn, it usually means there is decaying debris below the soil surface. See above for treatment.

tenance requirements. The grass can be planted from sprigs or seed. The fertility and soil pH requirements are considerably lower than most grasses, and it requires less mowing as well. Its tolerance to most turf diseases and response to water during droughty conditions are other desirable traits. Sometimes centipedegrasses' low maintenance requirements give the homeowner a false sense of security in that the turf is often neglected which results in inadequate maintenance. In some cases, it is managed like high maintenance grasses. Either attitude leads to mismanagement problems which results in the decline of the turf. Each spring many Georgia homeowners encounter a problem with centipedegrass called centipede decline. Normally, lawns of this grass grow quite well until the third to sixth year after planting. After this time, areas in some lawns may fail to grow or 'green-up' in the spring or summer.''

To prevent decline take the middle course. Neither under or over-fertilize. Don't allow thatch to build up. Mow no higher than 1 to 1½ inches.

Lawns in Florida

Lawn growing is different in Florida compared to many other areas of the South, hence our special focus here.

Many different grasses are available to Florida lawn growers: bahiagrass, bermudagrass, carpetgrass, centipedegrass, St. Augustinegrass, and zoysiagrass. Of these only bahia, common bermuda, carpet, centipede, and *Zoysia japonica* can be started from seed. (The remaining grass types must be started vegetatively.) The best time to seed is during the spring and summer months — April through September. This is the time of year when conditions are most favorable for germination and growth of warm-season grasses. In northern Florida, young grass seedlings may winter-kill if planted too late in the fall. Spring and summer seeding also takes advantage of Florida's rainy season, so the need for irrigation is reduced.

St. Augustinegrass is by far the most popular and commonly planted grass in Florida. It grows throughout the state and is especially well adapted to coastal areas.

Advantages of St. Augustinegrass.
St. Augustinegrass will grow in many types of soil, from pure sand or muck to the shell and marl soil of southern Florida. It will persist on both wet and dry sites, and has good salt and shade tolerance. When properly maintained, St. Augustinegrass produces

an attractive, dark green lawn that is very tough, withstanding considerable wear.

Some disadvantages. St. Augustinegrass is not perfect, of course. Its biggest problem is susceptibility to chinch bugs. They can be especially active when the weather is dry and hot, (see page 69).

St. Augustinegrass must be established by sod, sprigs, or plugs, rather than by seed. These establishment methods entail somewhat greater cost and effort.

Thatch may be another problem since St. Augustine is a fast-growing grass in Florida. For this reason, it requires medium to high levels of maintenance, including frequent mowing, medium-to-high fertilization, and periodic control of pests.

Varieties. There are six varieties of St. Augustinegrass that are generally available. The best are briefly mentioned on page 15; the following are more detailed descriptions.

'Roselawn' is primarily a pasture grass. It will make a very coarse, open sod and is not recommended for home lawn use. It is very similar to common St. Augustinegrass.

'Bitter Blue' is an improved selection which makes an excellent home lawn. It has an even, dark green color and leaves are shorter and closer set, which produces a particularly dense lawn if well maintained.

'Floratine' is similar to 'Bitter Blue' but is finer textured and produces a lower growing, more dense sod. If available, use *certified* 'Floratine.' A blue certification tag should accompany the sod, guaranteeing its purity.

'Scotts 1081' is vigorous and fine textured and will make an attractive lawn if properly cared for.

'Floratam' is available from certified sod growers and also produces a high-quality lawn. Prime advantages over the others is resistance to chinch bugs and SAD virus (see page 77). 'Floratam,' however, is not as fine textured or low growing as 'Floratine.'

Fertilizing. For northern Florida lawns, apply a complete fertilizer such as a 24-4-8, 21-4-4, or similar formula in both spring and fall for minimum maintenance.

An optimum program for northern Florida requires fertilizer applications March, May, July, and September. More fertilizer is needed in the southern part of the state, primarily because of the longer growing season.

Many factors usually combine to cause a poor lawn. Lack of fertilizer is by far most common. Other problems,

such as lack of weed control, mowing too low, to much shade, or drought. Usually it is easier to correct specific problems and apply a good cultural program to the existing lawn.

An optimum fertilization program for St. Augustinegrass in southern Florida includes fertilizer applications every other month. Follow label directions as to amounts and temperature restrictions.

Pests and disease. Chinch bugs are the most damaging insect pest. Sod webworms, armyworms, and mole crickets may also damage St. Augustinegrass. See pages 66 to 72.

Brown patch and grey leaf spot are the two most serious diseases. Occasionally, dollar spot, *Helminthosporium* leaf spot, and rust are problems. Nematodes may be a problem if growth is poor and other treatments such as fertilizing, bring no response. See pages 73 to 77.

Cautions

Read the label every time you spray or dust and pay attention to cautions and warnings. Mix sprays on a solid level surface to lessen spillage. Avoid spilling pesticides on the skin or clothing and wash exposed areas thoroughly with soap and water. Do not eat or smoke while spraying. Keep all chemicals out of reach of children. Store them in a locked cabinet or high on a shelf. Set aside a special set of mixing tools, measuring spoons, and graduated measuring cups. Use them for measuring and mixing sprays only. Be sure to keep all chemicals in their original, labeled containers. Store lawn fertilizers combined with weed killers, separately from garden fertilizers to prevent accidental misuse.

Let's say it again

There are many descriptive terms in this book. Many hold such importance, they should be explained and described again and again. *Aeration* and *compaction* are two such terms that every lawn keeper should engrave on stone.

Compaction can be caused by children playing on a wet lawn. Heavy machinery driven across a lawn forces air out and can compact soil. Paths across a lawn will also compact the soil, drive air out, and will often kill the grass.

You can get air into the soil, (aerification), by the use of an aerator which extracts plugs of soil from the lawn, allowing air to reach the root zone. The best time to aerify is when the lawn is actively growing.

Index

Tables and conversions

The lawn keeper is asked to be a measurer in almost every operation — "Apply 2# of nitrogen per 1000 square feet," "Mix two tablespoons per gallon," "Spread two or three inches of organic matter over the soil." "Determine the area of your lawn," "Add lime if soil tests show the need." In these directions we find the elements "How much," "How wide," "How long."

So you are about to measure the area of your lawn. Once the area is measured write it down for future reference.

Charts and tables index

There are many charts and tables distributed throughout this book. All have been designed to simplify and categorize the sometimes technical information that is needed to understand lawn growth and lawn care.

How many square feet?

Irregular shapes
(within 5% accuracy)

Measure a long (L) axis of the area. At every 10 feet on the length line measure the width at right angles to the length line. Total all widths and multiply by 10.

Area = (A$_1$ A$_2$ + B$_1$ B$_2$ + C$_1$ C$_2$ etc.) x 10

A = (40' + 60' + 32') x 10
A = 132' x 10'
A = 1,320 square feet

Unusual shapes

Calculations can be made by sections and totaled.

In this case calculate and add together:

Area of triangle
Area of rectangle
One-half area of circle
TOTAL = square feet in area

Circle
Area = πR^2
π = 3.14
R = Radius
A = 3.14 x 20' x 20'
A = 1,256 square feet

Square or rectangle
Area = LW
L = Length
W = Width
A = 90' x 60'
A = 5,400 square feet

Triangle
Area = 0.5 BH
B = Base
H = Height
A = 0.5 x 60' x 120'
A = 3,600 square feet

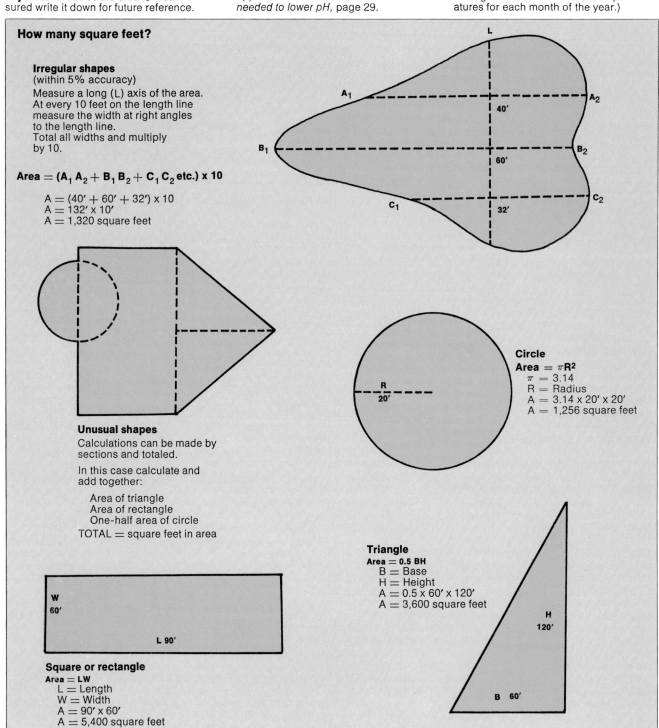